# PUBLIC PORTS FOR INDIANA
## A History of the Indiana Port Commission

Indiana Historical Collections
Volume 55

ISSN 0073-6880
ISBN 1-885323-54-9

# PUBLIC PORTS FOR INDIANA
## A History of the Indiana Port Commission

*Ralph D. Gray*

*with an Epilogue by Bill Beck*

Published in association with the
Indiana Port Commission

Indiana Historical Bureau
Indianapolis 1998

# CONTENTS

# PREFACE AND ACKNOWLEDGMENTS

The Indiana Port Commission is a young organization, but its roots stretch back to the earliest days of Indiana history. As early as the 1830s came the first attempts to secure a deepwater public port for northwestern Indiana, but not until the 1930s did various commercial groups and then the state of Indiana get involved in a concerted effort to build a public port at or near the point where Burns Ditch, a drainage channel, enters Lake Michigan. This led to the establishment, in 1939, of the Indiana Board of Public Harbors and Terminals, essentially an under-funded fact-finding and lobbying group. In 1961, the Indiana Board of Public Harbors and Terminals was succeeded by the Indiana Port Commission, a more powerful and, eventually, well-funded body, which, over the course of the past thirty years, has constructed and now operates three public ports. The Port of Indiana/Burns International Harbor is located on Lake Michigan at Portage in Porter County; the Southwind Maritime Centre is located on the Ohio River near Mount Vernon in Posey County; and the Clark Maritime Centre, also on the Ohio, is at Jeffersonville in Clark County.

These three ports, constructed in the 1960s (Burns), the 1970s (Southwind), and the 1980s (Clark), now constitute major economic assets of the state of Indiana and are poised and ready to make valuable contributions to the economic development of the state in the years to come. Although each port in its own way was born amid controversy, each has survived, and together these "ports of promise," as they were designated in a press report, are able to carry out the functions for which they were established in the first place. Moreover, the Indiana Port Commission, tempered by the political flames through which it has passed during the last three decades, is also ready to move ahead with the ongoing tasks of completing the ports' infrastructure, aiding the industrial development of lands located within port boundaries, and seeking new marketing and trade opportunities.

It is appropriate that the Indiana Port Commission saw fit to authorize this study upon the occasion of its thirtieth anniversary. Many participants, both governmental and industrial, associated with the stirring events surrounding the planning and building of the three ports, particularly the first one, were still able to provide useful first-hand accounts of their experiences and perceptions; at the same time, the construction phase of the Port Commission's history is clearly over, and the shake-down cruise has been completed. Now, as the commission enters a new developmental phase, it is time to take stock of what has been accomplished and to focus on new goals, particularly as they were articulated in a strategic planning document adopted by the commission in 1989.

I was first approached to do this study of the Port Commission by a colleague, whose son worked at the commission. This contact in turn led to discussions with William H. Keck, a long-time member of the commission and, in 1989, its chairman. I was eager to undertake the project. It would not have been possible, however, without the considerable support of members of the commission staff, beginning with Executive Director Frank G. Martin, Jr. I am particularly grateful to William Friedman, the commission's former director of planning and grants, for the initial contact and for many favors thereafter, including joint trips to all of the ports and introductions to the port directors and staff members at these distant points. I also gained many helpful insights regarding public ports generally, and the Indiana ports specifically, from discussions with John L. Coulter, the affable and knowledgeable former director of marketing, Jeanene Green, former commission controller, and Joy McCarthy, former director of industrial development.

One of the special joys of doing a project of this type is the opportunity to share in the reminiscences of those involved, in one way or another, in its history. I will long remember the day I spent with Chairman Keck and former commissioner Robert M. Schram at Mr. Keck's home in Mount Vernon. There, on property overlooking the serene Ohio River, I was able to discuss, with men whose combined service on the Indiana Port Commission totaled forty-two years, events and individuals associated with the history of the commission. I also benefited from briefer interviews with several of the sitting commissioners, former commissioner and chairman Quentin A. Blachly, and, on the political side, from discussions about the port with Lieutenant Governor Frank L. O'Bannon, former governor Matthew E. Welsh, Judge S. Hugh Dillin, James A. Farmer (who also supplied me with helpful documents), and Gordon Engelhart. Others with whom I was not able to speak, nevertheless, supplied me with their written recollections. Particularly worthy of mention in this regard are transportation economist David G. Abraham, a former consultant to the commission, and Thomas E. Dustin, a leading environmentalist in Indiana from the 1950s to the present. I am also grateful to Justin E.

Walsh and the staff of the Indiana State Archives for repeated favors while I searched through Indiana Board of Public Harbors and Terminals and Port Commission records in their safekeeping.

It should be noted that most of the pages in this study, and the above paragraphs, were initially composed in 1990 for anticipated publication at the time of the Indiana Port Commission's thirtieth anniversary in 1991. For various reasons, publication has been delayed far beyond what any of us involved in the process could have expected, but an advantage of that delay has been improvement in the narrative and, especially, in its documentation. The author is grateful for the considerable time and labor expended by Pamela J. Bennett, director of the Indiana Historical Bureau, and Historical Bureau editors Alan Conant and Janine Beckley on this project. Alan F. January and the staff of the Indiana State Archives have continued their invaluable help. I also wish to acknowledge the contribution of Bill Beck, a consultant and public relations expert with the commission, for the Epilogue on the 1990s. This addition goes a long way, it seems to me now (nearly seven years later), toward validating my upbeat and sanguine predictions about the future of the ports.

I am also grateful for the continued interest and support of Frank G. Martin and members of his staff at the Indiana Port Commission. Indeed, the Port Commission is a remarkable asset to the state of Indiana, and as the Port Commission enters its fifth decade of service, which coincides with the beginning of the twenty-first century, it is well equipped to continue making major contributions to the well-being of the state and all of its people.

Ralph D. Gray
Indianapolis, Indiana
March 21, 1997

Governor Frank L. O'Bannon addresses a gathering of employees of the Indiana Port Commission and companies located at the Clark Maritime Centre on the docks on October 2, 1997. The employees had recently completed a "Heart Walk" for the American Heart Association–wearing special T-shirts as pictured in the foreground. Governor O'Bannon was on a statewide tour promoting volunteerism.

# FOREWORD

## by Governor Frank L. O'Bannon

Some of my earliest childhood memories are of the barge traffic on the Ohio River. I can remember crossing the Kentucky and Indiana bridge from New Albany to Louisville and watching the string of barges glide underneath. For a close-up view of the barges and their big river tugs, my dad would take me to Dam 44 near Leavenworth, Indiana.

I grew up in Corydon, and the Ohio River was our front yard. Generations of O'Bannons have been river people, and we have instinctively understood the critical roles that Indiana's waterways and ports play in moving Hoosier goods to domestic and world markets.

True, no oceans lap our boundaries. But Indiana is blessed with ample waterborne trade, thanks to the Ohio River, which flows past our southern boundary, and Lake Michigan, which washes our northwestern shore. Hoosier farmers and manufacturers are able—and have been for decades—to utilize the state's waterways, shipping agricultural commodities and manufactured goods south on the Ohio and Mississippi rivers to New Orleans on the Gulf of Mexico and east via the Great Lakes/St. Lawrence Seaway System to Europe and the world.

Professor Ralph Gray's fascinating summary of maritime development in Indiana is a book that all Hoosiers would do well to read. The dream of public ports for Indiana, as Professor Gray points out, goes back more than a century. Hoosier politicians and business executives have long been convinced of the value of waterborne transportation to move the state's goods to expanding global and domestic markets. But it is only in the postwar era that the state and private enterprise have succeeded in building Indiana's modern system of three public ports and their accompanying modern infrastructure.

The struggle to build Indiana's International Port near Portage in Porter County is a particularly gripping story—and one that is near and dear to my heart. As a state senator and a member of the Senate Budget Committee and the Senate Finance Committee, my father, Bob O'Bannon, was a strong supporter of the new port on Lake Michigan in both the 1963 and 1965 sessions.

My father helped broker the 1963 deal that helped garner northern Indiana support for the construction of bridges across the Ohio at

Mauckport and Cannelton and the 1965 deal that helped swing southern Indiana support behind the creation of the International Port at Burns Harbor. Later in his career, my father supported the construction of ports at Jeffersonville and Mount Vernon on the Ohio River.

My predecessors in this office deserve much credit for creating and encouraging development of a public port system that is second to none in the United States.

The late Governor Matthew E. Welsh had the vision and perseverance to fight entrenched political interests in Illinois to site a deepwater port at Burns Ditch in northwestern Indiana. When the port at Burns Harbor opened in 1970, just over a decade after the opening of the St. Lawrence Seaway, Indiana finally had its outlet to the sea.

Otis Bowen presided over the opening of Indiana's window to the world on the Ohio River. Bob Orr, as lieutenant governor and governor, was a tireless promoter of the development of Clark Maritime Centre and Southwind Maritime Centre, Indiana's state-of-the-art Ohio River ports. The Ohio River now transits more waterborne commerce annually than passes through the Panama Canal.

Evan Bayh, my immediate predecessor in the governor's office, was also a champion of public port development in Indiana, which has helped create a national model for other states as they look to develop a new maritime agenda.

My hat is off to all those who had the vision to develop the three ports. The ports have enhanced greatly the state's economic growth position.

Today, Indiana's International Port, and the two public ports on the Ohio River are thriving centers of maritime commerce. More than $2 billion in private investment has helped create 5,700 family-wage jobs in Indiana. Indiana's public ports are a tribute to the vision of an earlier generation of Indiana government and business executives, and their story is admirably told in the pages of Ralph Gray's history of Indiana's ports.

# The Public Ports of Indiana

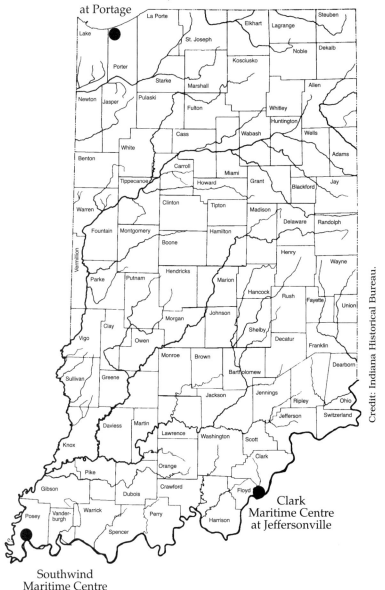

Indiana's International Port/Burns Harbor
at Portage

Southwind
Maritime Centre
at Mount Vernon

Clark
Maritime Centre
at Jeffersonville

Credit: Indiana Historical Bureau.

## CHAPTER 1

# Waterways in Indiana History

Water transportation has always been a part of Indiana history. Indian populations for thousands of years utilized the area now known as Indiana and usually settled along streams and rivers. These waterways provided avenues for trade and travel. The first Europeans to arrive in the area also relied on waterways, and the portages between them, for movement of people and supplies.

The first French outposts established in the eighteenth century in the Indiana area were on rivers. Fort des Miamis (the future site of the city of Fort Wayne) was located where two rivers—the St. Joseph and St. Mary's—converge to form a third, the Maumee, which connects northeastern Indiana with Lake Erie. Two other forts were built along the Wabash River. Fort Ouiatenon was located south of modern-day West Lafayette, and the fort at Vincennes was located north of the confluence of the Wabash and Ohio rivers. These eighteenth-century French forts were eventually relinquished to Great Britain as a result of the French and Indian War (1754-1763). The British foothold in the Ohio Valley was brief and uneventful with the exception of George Rogers Clark's dramatic capture of the British Fort Sackville at Vincennes in 1779.

Americans secured title to the land including Indiana by the Treaty of Paris in 1783. Then Congress, under the Articles of Confederation, moved quickly to adopt laws for the survey and sale of the land and a unique and farsighted plan for its governance. The Northwest Ordinance (1787) provided for the eventual equality of the states carved from the area north and west of the Ohio River; it also established a fundamental right: free travel on the navigable waterways of the West. The fourth article of the ordinance provides that "The navigable Waters leading into the Mississippi and St. Lawrence, and carrying places between the same shall be common highways, and forever free . . . without any tax, impost or duty therefor."[1]

The Northwest Ordinance also provided for three to five states to be established within the limits of the Northwest Territory. Between the western edge of Pennsylvania and the Mississippi River, two vertical lines were drawn at what became the east and west borders of Indiana, thereby yielding three territories. When two additional territories were formed, a horizontal line, between Lake Erie and the Mississippi River that touched the southern tip of Lake Michigan, divided the territories west of Ohio into four administrative units: Indiana and Michigan territories east of Lake Michigan, and Illinois and Wisconsin territories west of the lake.

In 1800, when the United States Congress organized the Indiana Territory, it was a vast region containing everything between the Mississippi River and what became, in 1803, the state of Ohio. Congress permitted formation of a separate Michigan Territory in 1805 and a separate Illinois Territory (including Wisconsin) in 1809. By 1809, Indiana's borders approximated their current locations; the Ohio River formed the entire southern and southeastern boundary line, the Wabash River formed the extreme southwestern boundary, and the tip of Lake Michigan touched Indiana at its northwest corner.

The only significant modification in these boundaries came at the time of Indiana statehood in 1816. Congress moved the border between Indiana and Michigan ten miles north, thereby giving Indiana a portion of the Lake Michigan shoreline and the possibility of a port on the lake. The Indiana Enabling Act, adopted by Congress on April 19, 1816, located the state's northern boundary along "an east and west line, drawn through a point ten miles north of the southern extreme of Lake Michigan." The credit for this achievement apparently goes to Jonathan Jennings, Indiana's territorial representative in Congress. This action added approximately 1,100 square miles to the state.[2]

As Indiana was achieving statehood, other states were trying to address their transportation problems. The War of 1812 had dramatized the inadequacy of the rudimentary roads and unimproved rivers, which were unable to meet the country's transportation needs. Consequently, in 1816, Congress attempted to adopt a national program for roads and canals built at federal expense, which was based on an elaborate plan that had been set forth by Secretary of the Treasury Albert Gallatin in 1808. President James Madison (1809-1817) vetoed the bill, citing constitutional problems.

The state of New York, however, proceeded on its own, building and then operating the stunningly bold and successful Erie Canal, which stretched approximately 368 miles across the state linking the Atlantic coast (via the Hudson and Mohawk rivers) with the Great Lakes at Buffalo. The Erie Canal was begun in 1817 and completed eight years later at a cost of approximately $7,000,000. It transformed the transportation capabilities of New York and served as a model for countless other states, including Indiana, eager to transform their own economies by improved transportation networks.[3]

In 1827, only two years after the New York waterway was completed, Indiana received a large land grant from the federal government for its major canal enterprise. This canal, known as the Wabash and Erie, was begun in 1832, satisfying one condition of the land grant that construction begin within five years. The first section completed was opened between Fort Wayne and Huntington in 1835. The waterway was extended to Lafayette in 1843; that same year its eastward leg joined Ohio's Miami and Erie Canal at Defiance enroute to its eastern terminus at Toledo and Lake Erie. The original western terminus of the canal had been changed in 1836 from Lafayette to Terre Haute. From Terre Haute, a proposed Cross-Cut Canal was to extend southeastward to Port Commerce,[4] a planned industrial and commercial center near Worthington, where it was to join the Central Canal connecting Peru on the upper Wabash River with Evansville on the Ohio River by way of Indianapolis.

These waterways and other improvements were part of the Internal Improvements Act passed in 1836 by the Indiana General Assembly. The program proved to be too ambitious for the state; inexperience and mismanagement were but two of the reasons for failure. The major factor was general financial distress during the late 1830s. The "Panic of 1837" broadened into national depression in 1839, forcing the state to abandon all of its internal improvement projects by 1841, except for the Wabash and Erie Canal. The state retained this project, believing the federal land grant of 1827 obligated it to do so.[5]

In 1847, an arrangement with the state's creditors transferred the canal, and the land grant, to them. The bondholders accepted the canal as payment for fifty percent of the debt, but they also accepted the obligation to complete the canal to Evansville. The Terre Haute-Port Commerce section replaced the Cross-Cut Canal, and the Port Commerce-Evansville section replaced the lower Central Canal, which had been abandoned in 1839 and never completed. A three-member board of trustees—two elected by the bondholders and one appointed by the governor of Indiana—was responsible for the additional construction and for maintenance and operation of the canal when it was completed between Lake Erie and the Ohio River in 1853.[6]

For a time, the Wabash and Erie Canal prospered under the dedicated management of its trustees, particularly long-time members Charles Butler (1847-1874) and Thomas Dowling (1850-1874). They set high standards of performance for all employees and gave close attention to every detail of the enterprise. Efficient maintenance and operation of the canal on its upper divisions, from Terre Haute to Toledo, was coupled with new attentiveness to construction problems on its lower divisions, from Terre Haute to Evansville. Canal earnings reached their highest point in 1852, a year before the canal reached Evansville and the Ohio River. In 1853, Lake Erie and the Ohio River were linked by the longest canal—approximately 453 miles—ever built in the United States. A waterway like this had been the dream of such diverse men as George Washington and DeWitt Clinton[7] and of countless others after them; now it was a reality.

Unfortunately for canal promoters, however, railroads were also a reality in Indiana in the 1850s. Soon, virtually every mile of canal was paralleled by the rival system. The Wabash and Erie trustees closed the portion of their canal below Terre Haute in 1860, and activity on the remainder of the line ceased fourteen years later. Water transport was far from dead, but the Wabash and Erie Canal experience indicated that the day of the towpath and animal-powered barges had passed. Nationally, the only canals that survived were the ones advantageously situated and capable of being expanded into barge and ship canals suitable for mechanically powered vessels.

There was remarkable growth of railroads during the 1850s. On the national level, total trackage spurted from approximately 9,000 to more than 31,000 miles; on the state level, the increase was even more dramatic, jumping from barely 200 miles in 1850 to approximately 2,000 miles in 1860. New rail lines combined to create the first great intersectional links between Atlantic coast cities and the Great Lakes-Ohio River area. Vast networks of routes radiated from such major rail centers as Chicago and Indianapolis, where the nation's first combined or "union" station serving all railroads entering the city was erected in 1852-1853.[8] In the following decade, despite the disjuncture of the Civil War, the first of the transcontinental railroads provided connections all the way to the Pacific coast. Soon railroads dominated the economies, and perhaps the politics, of many eastern states.

Water transportation declined precipitously, especially during the final quarter of the nineteenth century. Traffic dropped sharply on even the most advantageously located canals in the country, such as the Erie in New York and the Chesapeake and Delaware in Maryland and Delaware. Others, less stable to begin with, such as the Wabash and Erie in Indiana, disappeared completely. Similarly, inland waterway traffic also declined. Tonnage figures plummeted on the Ohio River, successively the carrier of westering pioneers, flatboats, keelboats, and then steamboats laden with goods destined for New Orleans and world markets. Traffic losses were even greater on the Mississippi River; in 1880, two-thirds of the cotton received in New Orleans arrived by boat; in 1910, only ten percent arrived by boat. For the nation as a whole, "river traffic measured in ton-miles amounted to only two percent of the railway traffic in 1925."[9]

So thorough was railroad domination, even by the 1880s, that Congress acted, in 1887, to establish an Interstate Commerce Commission, designed to regulate railroad freight rates and prohibit discriminatory practices. Competition from waterborne carriers no longer served to keep rates "reasonable." Only on the Great Lakes, where bulk commodities such as coal, grain, lumber, and iron ore were moved in large quantities, did water transport increase during the late nineteenth century. Lake tonnage stood at 671,000 in 1865, reached the 1,000,000 mark in 1890, and stood at nearly 3,000,000 tons by 1915. The lake fleet in 1920 exceeded 600 vessels, many of which were as large or larger than ocean-going ships. A substantial price differential prevailed in favor of the lakers on the ton-mile rates for commodities moving on the Great Lakes.[10]

As the twentieth century dawned, there was a general renewal of public interest in water transportation. Eastern business interests sought federal funds for building or improving, and operating, a network of canals and intracoastal waterways. Led by President Theodore Roosevelt (1901-1909), conservationists, believing that water transportation was clean and efficient, joined the effort. Two federal waterways commissions, one appointed by Roosevelt and the other by his successor, President William H. Taft (1909-1913), served to focus public attention on both the Atlantic and Gulf intracoastal waterway systems, and on general waterway improvements. Completion of the Panama Canal and the dangers of coastal shipping during World War I also served to stimulate waterway modifications to facilitate increased shipping.

Along the Ohio River, where desultory improvements were made by the U.S. Army Corps of Engineers after 1885, activity picked up noticeably after the turn of the century. In 1906, the federal Rivers and Harbors Board recommended building several dozen locks and dams and establishing a nine-foot channel over the Ohio River's entire length from Pittsburgh to Cairo. This plan, carried out between 1910 and 1929, included the construction of forty-six lock and dam structures. Upon its completion, Ohio River traffic exceeded 23,000,000 tons, up seven-fold from the 1915 figure and almost twice what the engineers had estimated.[11]

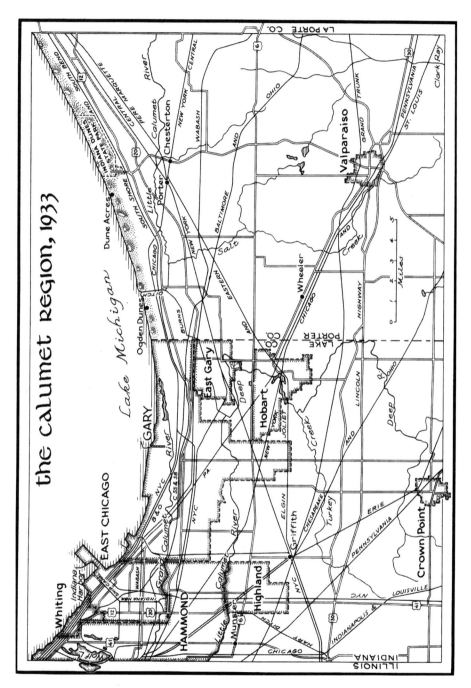

Credit: Powell A. Moore, *The Calumet Region: Indiana's Last Frontier* (Indianapolis: Indiana Historical Bureau, 1959), following 336.

# CHAPTER 2

# Developments in Northwest Indiana

Interest in an Indiana deepwater port during the 1920s and 1930s coincided with a national trend of further improvements to commercial water resources. Given the ongoing Ohio River improvements, attention focused on finding ways for Indiana to participate more fully in the shipping activity on Lake Michigan. Indiana was the only state bordering Lake Michigan without a public port. Inland Steel used a private industrial facility, known as Indiana Harbor, at East Chicago; the United States Steel Company in Gary had Buffington Harbor for receiving and shipping ore and steel; the Michigan City harbor, with limited channel depth and few facilities for handling large shipments, served primarily a fishing and recreational boating clientele.[1]

There had been slight industrial or commercial activity in the Indiana counties fronting Lake Michigan during the nineteenth century. The most important economic activity was agriculture, conducted well back from the sand-swept shores of the lake and marshlands surrounding the sluggish rivers that paralleled the shoreline. It seemed then that John Tipton's remark, made when the future Indiana senator first encountered the dunes areas in 1821, might be valid. This area, he predicted, "never will be of much service to our state."[2]

During the latter part of the nineteenth century, however, important events occurred leading toward the industrialization of Lake

County. There, in the extreme northwestern county of the state, George H. Hammond established his State Line Slaughter House in 1869, and a town named for him subsequently developed at the plant site. Later, an oil storage tank plant and a railroad car wheel factory, located to the east of Hammond, evolved into the town of East Chicago, which soon became home to steel fabricating plants. At this time, too, Standard Oil located a major oil refinery at Whiting. In 1901, the Inland Steel Company established a large mill.

The greatest boost to industrialization in the area came when United States Steel, the nation's first billion dollar corporation, decided to erect what became the largest steel mill in the world (the Gary Works) on an empty tract of land east of Hammond and East Chicago. The company quietly acquired some seven miles of shoreline and established its plant and a town named for its chairman, Elbert H. Gary, on the site in 1906. Its first "pour" occurred in 1909, and since that time the plant has produced more steel than any other in the world. The Gary Works also built its own private harbor.[3]

No public port suitable for handling general cargo existed at this time within the state of Indiana. Eastward from Gary the land remained undeveloped, agriculturally and industrially. As early as 1880, a materials company acquired a large tract of this seemingly low-value land as a source of sand, to be used in construction work, as fill material, or on beaches in Chicago. This business, the Consumers [Sand] Company, was profitable for a time, but sales sagged in the early years of the twentieth century, and the company sold portions of its property to National Steel's subsidiary, Midwest Steel, in 1929. Apparently National was interested in building a large steel plant at this location, but 1929 was not a propitious time for such ventures. The steel company waited.

One major development had already occurred—the completion of a drainage ditch, named after its most avid proponent, Randall W. Burns, a prosperous farmer and land developer. It had been his idea to drain much of the marshland surrounding the Little Calumet River east of Gary in order to render the land suitable for housing or industry. He easily found cosigners for the petition he presented to the county commissioners of Lake and Porter counties in 1908, who supported the plan and appointed a three-member drainage commission in 1909.

Opposition to the proposed "Burns Ditch" was soon heard from local farmers, the railroads, and a power company. Railroads, whose lands would be crossed by the proposed Burns Ditch, sought dam-

Burns Ditch, circa 1948; aerial view looking south from Lake Michigan. The attached note, perhaps written by George A. Nelson, refers to historical documents (circa 1930-1949) assembled for the Indiana Board of Public Harbors and Terminals.

THIS IS BURNS DITCH THE FIRST PROPOSED LOCATION OF THE PORT SITE LATER CHANGED TO LOCATION APPROX 1 MI. EAST –

THIS BOOKLET CONTAINS AN INDEX TO THE LARGE BOOK CONTAINING A NUMBER OF IMPORTANT HISTORICAL DOCUMENTS ages to cover the cost of new bridges required to carry their trains over the ditch. Litigation continued for a number of years, ending favorably for Burns Ditch in the United States Supreme Court in January 1917. The start of construction was delayed until 1923. Eventually completed in 1926, the eight-mile long Burns Ditch entered Lake Michigan near Ogden Dunes on land that had been purchased by Midwest Steel. The ditch, which drained some 400 square miles of marshland, gave both a geographic focus and a name to the port project that eventually was located a mile east of its mouth.[4]

Of significance, also, was the establishment of the Indiana Dunes State Park in Porter County, 1923-1925. This northwest Indiana location was identified as early as 1920 by Richard Lieber, director of the Indiana Department of Conservation, as a potential site for a state park: "It is plainly the duty of the State to rescue this land of unsurpassed beauty and protect it for all time to come." The federal government had already declined, despite some vigorous agitation by conservationists and others, to establish a national park there. As Lieber pointed out, there was no legal precedent for such federal action; the other national parks had been established either from lands already in the public domain or on lands donated to the government. Lieber noted, however, that there were ample reasons for the state to act:

> According to scientists our own Indiana Sand Dunes are the finest in the world. They . . . possess extremely interesting fauna and flora; offer unparalleled opportunities to observe the action of wind and its influence on the sand and plant life. The Lake Michigan beach is beautiful and . . . recreational uses are unlimited. The Dunes are poetic, they are beautiful, they are wonderful; they are just about the most beautiful and wonderful thing we have in the mid-west.

Lieber proposed a park with an eight-mile shoreline and a depth of one and a half miles. He anticipated no interference by the park with existing industrial development and even expansion; indeed, the park was important for that growth, he believed: "The Dunes are the only real outlet for the people of Chicago and Indiana on to Lake Michigan. They are the one big and last opportunity to furnish a great recreational outdoors for the millions of Chicago and Northern Indiana industrial centers. Their health value is enormous."[5]

Two essentials for obtaining the park were legal authority and money. In 1923, the Indiana General Assembly authorized the levy of a two-mill tax on each $100 of taxable property in Indiana for seven years in order to provide an estimated $1,000,000 for a park, although it would be scaled down from Lieber's original dream. The Indiana Dunes State Park was to contain some 2,000 acres of land spread out along three miles of shoreline. Several prominent private citizens, as well as United States Steel Corporation, raised a large portion of the initial money needed for the land purchase; the state appropriation, designated for park development, was used as it accumulated. The park marked significant preservation and recreational progress; its existence also blunted later protests for preservation of the dunes.[6]

In 1931, the arrival of George A. Nelson as manager of the Valparaiso Chamber of Commerce marked a significant point in the history of Indiana's lakeport.[7] Almost as soon as he arrived in Porter County, Nelson learned of longstanding efforts on the part of many there to have a public port in Indiana. Banker and developer Patrick W. Clifford encouraged Nelson's interest in the project. Together, in 1932, they drove to the lakefront location of the "old Consumers Sand property . . . which had been sandmined for more than 50 years." As Nelson recalled the event some forty-four years later, Clifford looked out over the water and said, "'There she is—Lake Michigan—pointed down into the heartland of the USA like a great finger into the bread basket of America.' Then he turned to me and said, 'As surely as we stand here, a great public port will be built in this area. Maybe not in our time, but let's see if we can make it happen.'"[8] This quiet conversation on the lakefront began Nelson's nearly fifty-year struggle on behalf of an Indiana deepwater port.

In 1930, a resolution offered by Congressman William R. Wood of Lafayette calling for a preliminary survey of a commercial port site in or near Burns Ditch had been adopted. Wood knew from attorney E. J. Freund, Valparaiso, that Midwest Steel, with immediate oversight of the steel company property at Burns Ditch, was interested in an investigation of the feasibility of a public harbor at that location and was willing to cooperate. Wood's resolution resulted in two reports submitted to the Chicago District Office of the U.S. Army Corps of Engineers in December 1931. One report was a survey of the development possibilities of the Calumet waterways by Colonel Arthur P. Melton. A second report, compiled by Major H. J. Wild without the benefit of a public hearing, indicated that a public port was not economically justified at that time because the benefits would accrue primarily to a single business (Midwest Steel). Despite its limited scope, the report by Wild bedeviled subsequent efforts to obtain positive recommendations for a public port in the Burns Ditch area for years to come.[9]

An essential task for Nelson, the Valparaiso Chamber of Commerce, and others interested in a public port was to get federal legislation authorizing a new study. If a favorable recommendation followed, federal participation in constructing the port could be sought. To this end the Valparaiso chamber formed a port committee (chaired by Clifford but directed primarily by Nelson), hired an engineer, William J. Venning, to gather data related to the port—both technical engineering studies and traffic projections, and set about enlisting political support. Frank W. Morton, an original member of the port committee, wrote to Indiana's entire congressional delegation, reporting on the committee's activities and asking for assistance. He suggested that success would mean not only many construction jobs but "at least one thousand men or more will be permanently employed and off the relief rolls."[10]

A major step forward came in 1935, when the Valparaiso group decided to broaden its base by inviting other civic and business organizations to join in the effort. They formed the Northern Indiana Industrial Development Association (NIIDA), in reality a single-purpose lobbying organization seeking a deepwater port for Indiana. Patrick W. Clifford continued as chairman of the larger group, which included chambers of commerce from Hammond on the west to Fort Wayne on the east and a number of other business and labor groups in Lake County. Nelson continued as secretary.[11]

Rather than promoting a harbor for the benefit of private industry, as some critics charged, the NIIDA wanted a truly public harbor, owned by an agency of the state and available to all. As the NIIDA stated in a historical review of events, one of its primary concerns from the outset was "to PREVENT the establishment of a private harbor at the mouth of Burns Ditch, in Porter County, which development would eliminate forever the last possible location for a public commercial harbor, and rob this State for all time of its last breathing point, an adequate outlet to the waters of the Great Lakes and St. Lawrence and Mississippi waterways." Already private interests had claimed the Indiana shoreline, consuming practically everything from the Illinois state line to the Michigan state line except for the land in the Indiana Dunes State Park. All of the tracts suitable for a port were gone, except for some three miles of undeveloped frontage, but even that was held by private industry, including the land on both sides of Burns Ditch.[12]

Another significant event for the eventual establishment of the port was the election of Charles A. Halleck to Congress in 1934. He remained for seventeen terms (1935-1969), becoming not only a vociferous champion of an Indiana port but also a major figure in the leadership of Congress. Halleck moved quickly to represent his district and promote its, and the state's, economic development. He recalled many times that among the first visitors at his office in Washington were port proponents, and he soon endorsed their efforts wholeheartedly.[13]

In 1935, Halleck sponsored a resolution calling upon the House Committee on Rivers and Harbors to review the Corps of Engineers' negative report on the Burns Ditch project, submitted by Major H. J. Wild in 1931. The resolution was adopted, and the Corps responded by scheduling a public hearing on the project for August 1935. While preparing for the hearing, Clifford and Nelson communicated with the new district engineer in Chicago, Lieutenant Colonel Donald H. Connolly, who mentioned a series of steps that needed to be taken in order to overcome the objections to the port brought forth in the Wild report.[14]

As a result, prior to the August 22 session, NIIDA representatives obtained a number of agreements and concessions from interested industrialists. Most importantly, Midwest Steel agreed to sell all of its land on the west side of Burns Ditch to bona fide industries at a price no greater than it had paid. The company also agreed to erect 1,000-foot long bulkheads on both sides of Burns Ditch, and pledged, immediately upon the start of public harbor construction, to begin construction of a multi-million dollar steel mill. Additionally, the company agreed to grant the necessary acreage for a public port to an appropriate state agency empowered to receive it, and to provide the necessary easements for highway and railroad access to the terminal.[15]

With these agreements and understandings in hand, the NIIDA confidently participated in the August 1935 proceedings. More than 200 people crowded into the hearing room in Chicago, led by Indiana Governor Paul V. McNutt (1933-1937) and a number of other state and federal officials, including several Indiana congressmen and both senators, as well as various business and labor representatives. H. L. Gray, assistant to the president of Midwest Steel, confirmed his company's pledges of support and listed the anticipated economic benefits of a port at Burns Ditch. Clarence Manion, the Indiana director of the National Emergency Council, testified that the project embodied the "highest ideals of the work-relief program" and would help restore normal business conditions in the area.[16]

Among the documents submitted by various interested parties to the Corps of Engineers at the public hearing were worksheets summarizing expected shipments, tonnage estimates, current freight rates, and the savings expected if a port existed. Letters and testimonials regarding the need for a port came from such firms as the Crisman Sand Company of Crisman, Indiana and the Aetna Sand and Gravel Company of Chicago. The latter reported the loss of former orders for thousands of tons from Michigan, Ohio, and Pennsylvania: after "the rise of freight rates we have lost it all. If a harbor was built, we no doubt could get most of our trade back by shipping by water." A similar report came from the McGill Manufacturing Company of Valparaiso, producer of ball bearings and other castings, which considered itself handicapped by prevailing rail rates and therefore limited in its market opportunities. The Indiana Steel Products Company of Chicago, which turned out approximately 1,000 tons of magnets annually, noted that all of its raw materials could be brought in by water, and perhaps half of its output would be shipped that way to eastern and northeastern markets. The Common Carriers Conference and the Motor Truck Association of Indiana also favored development of a public port at Burns Ditch, for reasons of both economy and safety. Some 400 trucks a day, carrying over 19,000,000 pounds of cargo, moved into the Chicago area. The truckers favored a less congested destination.[17]

The most detailed analysis came from Professor George W. Starr of the Indiana University School of Business and director of its Bureau of Business Research. Starr, a consultant to the NIIDA, reported on the existing waterborne traffic into the Calumet area: 14,000,000 tons of iron ore, 7,000,000 tons of limestone, 10,600,000 tons of coal, 85,000 tons of steel, and 100,000 tons of general, non-bulk cargo to Indiana Harbor, even though it did not have good port facilities. In addition, one-third of Chicago's transshipped grain— about 60,000,000 bushels a year—went eastward by water, even though most of Chicago's elevators were located on the Chicago River, its branches, and the Chicago drainage canal—all cluttered by seventy-eight bridges. Starr also listed smaller amounts of traffic in petroleum products, automobiles, trucks, and canned goods, and stated his belief that an increase in industry and traffic in other items would develop after the new port was built. To reinforce his latter point, Starr provided some historical perspective. Starr noted that "As late as 1880 less than three per cent of all the manufacturing in Indiana was done in Lake County; less than one per cent in Porter County." In 1930, Lake County accounted for one-third of Indiana's total manufacturing; Porter County remained at less than one percent. Starr concluded that a port in Porter County would produce industrial development similar to that in Lake County.[18]

Only one negative report was submitted. It came from Walter Mills, chairman of the River and Harbor Committee of the Chicago Real Estate Board, but there is evidence that he did not, in fact, speak for the board. Moreover, his opposition was counterbalanced by strong support from another Chicagoan involved in real estate, William J. Venning. Nelson has identified Venning as an important ally in the fight for Burns Harbor, and many letters from Venning regarding this matter indicate his activities over the years. Initially an engineer for the city of Chicago, he was also deeply involved in bringing industry into northwest Indiana. He saw the port as a vital cog in the process. Venning handled transactions when National Steel, through its subsidiary Midwest Steel, purchased its Burns Ditch property in 1929, and he represented the firm in its later real estate dealings in that area.[19]

All in all, the Chicago event was, as George Nelson recalled in 1976, "one hell of a hearing." Governor McNutt delivered a particularly strong statement of support, and seemingly things were "going well." According to Nelson, however, a silent but powerful "opposition was strong enough to get the district engineer . . . transferred out of there within a matter of hours."[20] Obviously, Nelson and others had fully expected Colonel Connolly to issue a report favorable to the project. According to the NIIDA statement, Connolly had privately assured port supporters that he intended to approve plans for the port, but he was abruptly transferred from Chicago to a west coast position and not allowed to make his report. Instead, the Acting District Engineer, Captain S. N. Karrick, issued the Corps' report that recommended no change from the findings in 1931. Karrick's report, as quoted in the NIIDA statement, concluded that "prospective general public benefits are insufficient to justify the cost of the improvement by the United States, so long as the production of steel is well below the capacity of existing plants."[21]

Bulging Port Commission files in the Indiana State Archives bear witness to the extensive preparations that went into the 1935 hearing, and suggest the momentary despair that followed the negative recommendation. The resources of the governor's office and the State Planning Board, as well as all-but-unanimous support from the state's congressional delegation had come to naught. Plans, suggested by Clarence Manion, state director for the National Emergency Council, for Works Progress Administration funds to assist in constructing the port also failed to materialize. It was to Manion, at any rate, that a momentarily dejected Nelson sent a copy of the Karrick

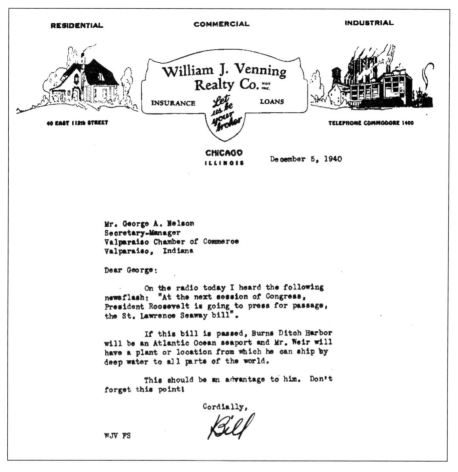

RESIDENTIAL          COMMERCIAL                    INDUSTRIAL

William J. Venning
Realty Co. INC.

INSURANCE     *Let us be your broker*     LOANS

46 EAST 112th STREET                        TELEPHONE COMMODORE 1400

CHICAGO
ILLINOIS          December 5, 1940

Mr. George A. Nelson
Secretary-Manager
Valparaiso Chamber of Commerce
Valparaiso, Indiana

Dear George:

On the radio today I heard the following
newsflash: "At the next session of Congress,
President Roosevelt is going to press for passage,
the St. Lawrence Seaway bill".

If this bill is passed, Burns Ditch Harbor
will be an Atlantic Ocean seaport and Mr. Weir will
have a plant or location from which he can ship by
deep water to all parts of the world.

This should be an advantage to him. Don't
forget this point!

Cordially,

Bill

WJV FS

E. T. Weir was chairman of National Steel, which was considering the construction of a steel mill at Burns Ditch. William J. Venning was a real estate agent in Chicago with an interest in the proposed Burns Ditch Harbor.

report. "This was an unpleasant surprise to me," he admitted, for a negative report was totally unexpected. Still, as he noted, "We are, of course, going to ask for an appeal before the Board of Engineers on Rivers and Harbors." Nelson then asked Manion to "appear and assist us in convincing that board that this project is not only a worthy project but is economically sound and should be built."[22]

The appeals board set March 16, 1936 as the rehearing date. Again a large and influential delegation presented the case for the port. The group submitted additional data and included forceful speakers, including Governor McNutt, both Indiana senators, and two congressmen representing different portions of northwest Indiana.[23]

The appeals hearing seemed to go very well. A hand-labeled document, "By Paul V. McNutt Mar 16, 1936 . . . " outlines the contents of McNutt's remarks to the Board of Engineers for Rivers and Harbors. There are, he began, three parts to our appeal—oral statements today, a statement from the NIIDA, and a report by a consulting engineer, sponsored by the State Planning Board. He then suggested that the Corps of Engineers' unfavorable reports of 1931 and 1935 were flawed in their basic premises: the signed agreements from Midwest Steel invalidate the 1931 findings, and those present here today invalidate the 1935 findings. They were not appealing, he emphasized, "for the benefit of any particular industry," but rather "in the hope that Indiana may gain a public terminal at this point." The other harbors in the vicinity were unsuited to current needs: the East Chicago Dock and Terminal Company is overloaded, Michigan City has limited space, the Gary and Buffington harbors are private, and it was "questionable whether the Chicago Harbor or Chicago River should longer operate because of its bridge problem and general congestion." McNutt concluded on a more philosophical note: "Along the southern end of Lake Michigan, the land is not fertile for a long distance south of the shore line. This poor territory has always been a burden on account of its small taxable value, but we feel that the time has come through this great development to lift this burden from the shoulders of its citizens."[24]

With the other speakers and the documents reinforcing these points, Nelson was optimistic at the conclusion of the day. He wrote to Clarence Manion in February 1936, "We have done our best to overcome every objectional [sic] point raised by the District Engineer and the Division Engineer." His assessment from hindsight, however, was that "we got tromped again" in the appeals process. The Board of Engineers reaffirmed Captain Karrick's negative report.[25]

Nevertheless, some progress had been made; moreover, Nelson had received some high level encouragement. Colonel Spalding, supposedly the "toughest" man on the board, talked to Nelson privately after the hearing and said, "Son, don't ever give up . . . . It [the port] is going to take place when the economic conditions warrant it but you are going to have to have steel in there. You can't do it without steel." Nelson also reported another informal, unofficial response from Captain Karrick, the acting district engineer at Chicago whose negative report in 1935 was so upsetting. Karrick suggested to Nelson sometime later that, despite the work and the interest of the people of Indiana, "you're not ever going to get this job done because we're not going to accept the word of your governor . . . or your highway commission chairman, or your planning commission, because you don't have a state agency to handle this harbor project. And until you do, you're never going to get to first base."[26]

Following the unfavorable appeals board ruling, Congressman Halleck again introduced legislation (House Resolution 7051) in 1936 and 1937 calling for a new survey of the Burns Ditch area. He was responding, in part, to the Board of Engineers' statement that there was probable future need for a public harbor in Indiana, but that "the selection of a site for such an improvement should be based on a comprehensive review of the whole available frontage." Consequently, the Halleck resolution, adopted as part of the Rivers and Harbors Act of 1937, called for a comprehensive survey of "the entire lake shore of the State of Indiana . . . with a view to the establishment of a commercial harbor and the most suitable site." The Corps of Engineers arranged for another public hearing in Chicago on November 9, 1937.[27]

At this time, opposition within the state of Indiana to a public harbor in the Burns Ditch area began to emerge. Other communities coveted a harbor for themselves, and First District Congressman William T. Schulte of Hammond, for example, switched from all-out support of the Porter County site to intimations that it would benefit one industry only, suggesting instead improvements in a Calumet River project in Lake County. Conservationists interested in preserving the dunes also began to speak out against the project. One such opponent, W. L. Phillips, wanted the entire dunes area saved for recreational purposes, warning U.S. Senator Sherman Minton and other politicians of the folly of obtaining jobs for a few when they could provide recreation for thousands. Other less flamboyant conservationists—among them the Indiana Academy of Science (1885), the Prairie Club (1908) in Chicago, and the National Dunes Park Association (1916)—favored preservation of the dunes for their unparalleled scientific value as well as their natural beauty.[28]

Not until 1944, for reasons associated with the onset and prosecution of World War II, did a report emerge from the Corps of Engineers regarding the 1937 hearings. Again it was negative, but it did contain one sentence of enormous significance. Paragraph 65 of this report stated that "The Burns Waterway site is the only one on the Indiana shore of Lake Michigan at which sufficient space is available for the type of general industrial and commercial harbor desired by local interests."[29] During later discussions and debates, many speakers had occasion to refer back to paragraph 65.

# CHAPTER 3

# The Indiana Board of Public Harbors and Terminals

In 1939, responding to effective lobbying efforts and the growing forcefulness of economic arguments, the state of Indiana established the Indiana Board of Public Harbors and Terminals (IBPHT). This act was a very important first step toward achieving a public harbor within Indiana's boundaries. Principal players, in and out of the legislature, involved in obtaining the act were John W. Van Ness, a Valparaiso businessman then serving his first term as state senator, and George Nelson, still employed by the Valparaiso Chamber of Commerce but reassigned to duties as a full-time lobbyist during the 1939 session of the Indiana General Assembly.

Nelson proved to be an effective advocate for the port and a continual irritation to those who opposed a port or who favored a port at a location other than Porter County. Particularly strong in their opposition to the port were the American Association of Railroads and Ed Wolfe, the lobbyist for the East Chicago and Hammond Chambers of Commerce who had been Nelson's boss at the Greater Lafayette Chamber of Commerce. Nelson took particular delight in outmaneuvering Wolfe, who "turned turkey gobbler red" when he learned that the IBPHT bills had been adopted. To counter the arguments of their opposition, the Northern Indiana Industrial Development Association (NIIDA) circulated among legislators a lengthy report outlining the history of the port project, the U.S. Army Corps of Engineers' activities regarding it in the 1930s, and a summary of the projected economic benefits to flow from the port.[1]

The bill to establish the IBPHT (House Bill 542, approved by the governor March 9, 1939) sailed through both houses of the legislature, but an appropriation for the board (House Bill 452, approved by the governor March 6, 1939) was a different matter. After the Senate failed to agree to the original $750,000 requested, or even to a $200,000 figure set in the House, the bill was bottled up in a conference committee on the budget with no resolution in sight. Lieutenant Governor Henry Schricker, president of the Senate, on the last evening of the session, appointed four or five different conference committees in succession trying to get the matter resolved. He was careful always to have at least one "port man" on these committees, but the difficulties persisted. Nelson, as the most visible target, was accused of delaying adjournment of the legislature and had become, he later asserted, "one of the most despised people in the world." He recalled that "We knew we were going to get some money, but we didn't know how much." Finally, at about 5 a.m., the Budget Committee emerged from its conference and asked the port advocates to accept $50,000 "to get your foot in the door." The port proponents agreed. As Nelson and John H. Stambaugh, president of the Valparaiso Chamber of Commerce, pointed out in a number of thank you notes sent to various Indiana legislators afterwards, the 1939 act was only the beginning, but it meant, in their view, that there would indeed be a public harbor in Indiana some day.[2]

The board thus created and minimally funded was to consist of five members appointed by the governor to four-year terms of office; the initial terms, however, included appointments for one, two, and three years. The board was to meet within thirty days after the members were selected, elect a chairman and a secretary from the membership, and meet thereafter as necessary. The power and duties of the board were limited, but included the authority to negotiate with the federal government regarding construction of a public harbor on Lake Michigan, to buy and sell land, condemning property if necessary, and to build, or join with the federal government in building, a public harbor or harbors. The board members were to be paid $10 a day, plus expenses, for each day actually spent on board duties, and the board was empowered to hire assistants. The first IBPHT officers were Dr. Malcolm B. Fyfe, Valparaiso, chairman; Clyde A. Walb, Fort Wayne, vice chairman; and Mark A. Moorman, Michigan City, secretary; the other members were Robert E. Wilhelm, Hammond, and Captain Ola F. Heslar, Indianapolis.[3]

Little attention was initially given to this agency partly, no doubt, because of the enormity of problems associated with fighting World War II and dealing with the economic and political dislocations that followed in its wake. The IBPHT, nevertheless, did some excellent work and accomplished much. Working quietly behind the scenes, the board's chief activities were to gather the geographical information and economic data required to prove the feasibility of an Indiana port on Lake Michigan. Among its very first actions was a petition to the Porter County commissioners that resulted in a name change for Burns Ditch—and the project—to Burns Waterway. The board also cultivated closer relations with H. L. Gray, an officer of Midwest Steel, a subsidiary of National Steel. Through Congressman Charles A. Halleck in 1940, the board sought a firm commitment from National Steel officials regarding plans for a plant in the Burns Waterway area. E. T. Weir, chairman of the parent company, declined to make the specific commitment desired, but he did indicate that when National Steel built its next plant, it would be in Porter County, Indiana. Soon thereafter, the state of emergency declared by President Franklin D. Roosevelt (1933-1945) suspended all civil works by the U.S. Army Corps of Engineers for the duration of World War II. As Heslar indicated, however, the IBPHT did not suspend its own activities but continued "to gain information on geography, lake currents, and dredging implications and to seek support from influential civil servants."[4]

The board was aware of the need for a connection between its planned harbor and the inland waterway system of the nation. That connection continues to be achieved by barges moving through the waters of Lake Michigan between the Burns and Calumet harbors. The first plan, however, was for a "public industrial harbor" via a canal between the Little Calumet and Grand Calumet rivers. There was even some discussion of attempting a "hook-up" with Michigan City via an interior canal, but the board formally rejected this idea in September 1939. Interested representatives from the Ohio River towns of Madison and Evansville were contacted by the board in 1940 on information-gathering trips. The efforts by Madison city officials and its Chamber of Commerce to establish a coal-shipping port were noted. A small public terminal (Mead-Johnson Terminal, 1931) already existed in Evansville, with cargo in excess of 400,000 tons in both 1937 and 1938. Members of the Valparaiso Chamber of Commerce tried to head off premature diversification by reminding the

Credit: D. White for Indiana Department of Natural Resources,
Division of Historic Preservation and Archaeology.

Mead Johnson River-Rail-Truck Terminal and Warehouse, built 1931;
aerial view in 1984 looking northwest along the Ohio River in Evansville.

board that it had been "created as a result of Valparaiso's efforts" at
the Burns Waterway site.[5]

Most importantly, though, the board was considering ways to get
the Army Corps of Engineers' negative reports reversed, working
through Senator Sherman Minton's office in Washington as well as
directly with the district engineer in Chicago, Captain Samuel N. Karrick. The engineer suggested that two things were needed: data
regarding tonnages and freight rates that would indicate a return-on-
investment of at least four percent plus annual maintenance costs
and evidence of additional local support that would make up any
shortfall. In March 1940, the board met with Senator Minton in his
Washington office, but by that time all public works activity had been
suspended. Although the board formally resolved in August 1940 to
"carry on" despite outside events, it voted in November of that year to
suspend regular meetings. At this same meeting, Secretary Moorman,
who had been investigating the development of the "St. Lawrence
Waterways," recommended that the board support that development.[6]

Not until October 1947 did the IBPHT resume its meetings, at
which time Heslar was elected chairman. The other board members,

all new, were J. W. Larrew, Valparaiso, elected secretary; Harry W. Frey, Michigan City; H. C. Dorman, Gary; and A. B. Weaver, Valparaiso. In 1949, Mark Moorman returned to the board, replacing Frey.[7] During the board's inactive period, only one notable port event had occurred—the Corps of Engineers submitted its preliminary examination report following the 1937 public hearing. As already noted in Chapter 2, this report did not recommend construction of a new lake port at that time, but it did contain the highly significant statement in paragraph 65 recognizing Burns Waterway as the only suitable site for the type of port being planned. In general, though, it was necessary to begin over again to build popular interest in the port project and to obtain the necessary support for it from Indiana's political leaders, beginning with Governor Ralph E. Gates, Jr. (1945-1949).

A series of meetings followed in the governor's office with industrial leaders and interested citizens. Indiana University President Herman B. Wells asked Professor George Starr to assist the board again in collecting and analyzing new economic data. The Indiana Economic Council and the IBPHT appointed consultant Kenneth L. Schellie to prepare a report on the potential value of the port project to the state as a whole. This flurry of activity led to the desired result—a new public hearing on the project set for July 19, 1949, in Gary. In March 1949, the Committee on Public Works, U.S. House of Representatives, called for a review of all previous reports on Burns Harbor, thereby authorizing Colonel W. P. Trower, the new district engineer for Chicago, to convene a hearing and listen to testimony from the IBPHT and others, both proponents and opponents. In his letter of invitation to scores of interested parties (it required seventeen pages of the hearing transcript to list them all), Trower stated the purposes of the hearing: to obtain information about the port, the reasons for the site chosen, the extent of the improvements planned, their impact upon the area, and the overall economic justification for the project.[8]

An impressive number and diversity of interests were represented at the hearing. The IBPHT set the tone of the proceedings by listing nine separate arguments for the port. The arguments, in part, noted that there was room for industrial development at the site in later years, and that the harbor, alone among potential sites, could accommodate a grain elevator that conformed to Indiana Farm Bureau specifications. The board also mentioned national security considerations and the need for a new harbor to handle increased shipping resulting from completion of the St. Lawrence Seaway. The IBPHT estimated the cost for the harbor project at just over $17,000,000, to be divided approximately equally between federal and state funds. The cost per year, over a twenty-year period, would be approximately $875,000, but the board estimated annual savings to shippers in excess of $8,000,000, yielding an impressive benefit-cost ratio of over nine to one.[9]

The board's position was supported by all but one of Indiana's congressional representatives, by Indiana's two recently elected senators, William E. Jenner and Homer E. Capehart, and by Governor Henry F. Schricker (1949-1953). The lone holdout, Thurman Charles Crook, U.S. representative from Michigan City, favored a port but wanted it in his district. Support also came from the Great Lakes Harbor Association; its representative pointed out that the Burns site had been selected following careful study (a controversial point) and that, in addition to port-to-port business within the Great Lakes, there would be a significant barge service between Burns and the inland waterways—indeed, barges from the nation's rivers already plied Lake Michigan, calling at Chicago and Milwaukee. He also indicated that there had been no significant Lake Michigan port development for two decades, and the opportunities for a modern port were considerable.[10]

Others who went on record on behalf of the port were the Indiana Department of Commerce, the Indiana Department of Conservation, the Indiana Economic Council, mayors and chambers of commerce of various northern Indiana cities, several labor groups, the Indiana Farm Bureau, and the Coal Trade Association of Indiana. This latter group pointed out that there were forty-five coal companies in Indiana, producing 23,000,000 tons of coal annually, an estimated 5,000,000 to 10,000,000 tons of which would utilize the Burns facility when available. Moreover, with ninety-eight percent of the state's known coal reserves still underground, there was no danger of exhausting the supply for roughly 2,000 years. Significantly, too, E. T. Weir, chairman of National Steel, endorsed the statement of the IBPHT and repeated his promise to make available to the state the land it needed for a port at the Burns site. Furthermore, he reaffirmed his company's plan to build a complete steel mill at the site, beginning with a finishing mill estimated to cost $20,000,000 to $25,000,000, to employ 1,000 workers, and to use 50,000 tons of slabs and coils a year shipped in from its mill in Michigan. Moving that tonnage by water rather than rail would save from $1,800,000 to $2,400,000 yearly.[11]

As expected, some in attendance at the hearing spoke out against the project. They included residents of Ogden Dunes, concerned about preserving the dunes and beaches in the area; the town board of Dune Acres, which stressed the need for recreational facilities

Children view a beach scene at Indiana Dunes State Park, circa 1940s.

there; the East Chicago Chamber of Commerce, which pointed instead to the virtues and expandability of Indiana Harbor at East Chicago and expressed doubts (valid at least until the 1990s, as it turned out) that significant coal traffic would develop at Burns; and various other individuals and groups expressed concern over the loss of the dunes environment.[12]

The IBPHT's careful preparation for the Gary hearing was convincing, however, and District Engineer Trower submitted a favorable preliminary report in 1950. He concluded that a harbor of the magnitude proposed by the state "appears" to be needed and economically justifiable, but he called for further investigation regarding its economic feasibility. The board's figures needed confirmation, but, when the board applied for the required funding of approximately $50,000 at yet another public hearing conducted by the Board of Engineers for Rivers and Harbors in Washington, D.C. in January 1951, its application was unsuccessful. The Korean conflict was a factor in delaying any federal action until 1954, at which time only a token $4,000 appropriation was made.[13]

Nevertheless, the testimony developed at the hearing in 1951 was significant. Some twenty-eight witnesses spoke before the seven-member Board of Engineers, including three Indiana congressmen and several labor, industry, and state of Indiana representatives. The technical purpose of the proceeding was to determine whether or not to approve the comprehensive survey recommended by the district engineer. Congressman Ray J. Madden of Gary spoke first, reviewing the recent history of the project and stressing the point that no truly public harbor existed in Indiana, and that no area along Lake Michigan between Illinois and Michigan other than Burns could accommodate the proposed facility. Congressman Halleck, in whose district the proposed port was located and whose enthusiasm for it never wavered, followed Madden to the speaker's stand. He reviewed his record of support during the sixteen years he had been in Congress, and was both eloquent and passionate in insisting that Burns represented the state's last chance for a great public harbor on Lake Michigan. The third congressman to speak, Shepard J. Crumpacker of South Bend, stated his objections to the project, suggesting that Indiana's existing harbors, including the one at Michigan City, were sufficient, and dwelling at some length upon, in his view, the ridiculous notion that extensive coal traffic would develop at Burns in the near future.[14]

When the IBPHT was called upon to present its statement, Secretary Larrew (in Heslar's absence) assured the Board of Engineers first of all that the Indiana board wanted all views aired. He urged that those who favored reserving the Burns Waterway land as a natural wildlife sanctuary or a recreational area should be heard, but informed the Corps of Engineers that the land in question had been owned since 1880 by industry, and that its natural beauty had been despoiled by the removal of hundreds of thousands of cubic yards of sand over the years. He also pointed to the existence of the Indiana Dunes State Park, which preserved a three-mile section of the Indiana shoreline to the east of the Burns site. The board's brief printed statement, which Larrew had summarized, concluded with a map of the area, a photograph showing the sand removal site, and a transcript of a Hammond *Times* editorial that underscored most of the points the board wanted to bring to the attention of the Corps of Engineers.[15]

The Hammond *Times* editorial first noted that the Corps of Engineers had postponed its decision regarding Burns Waterway until it could study the letters of protest that had come in after the Gary hearing in July 1949 and the district engineer's favorable recommendation early in 1950. One such protest had come from a recently formed Indiana Dunes Preservation Council, which "proposes an 8,000 acre federal memorial recreational park in the area earmarked for an industrial harbor." The paper responded with the suggestion that Lake Michigan was not only a boon to lovers of nature and sports-minded vacationists, but also played a vital economic role, and concluded:

> If the Calumet region is to continue to expand it must have additional harbor facilities to attract new industry. . . . It is inconceivable that all the thought, sweat and toil that has gone into the long-range planning of the . . . Burns Ditch harbor can be swept aside by a bar[r]age of letters from no doubt well-intentioned but uninformed people. . . . After this needed harbor has been built—as we trust it will—there will still be thousands of acres of dunelands for the new society to preserve.[16]

The flurry of activity in 1949-1951, along with many welcome expressions of support like the one quoted above, seemed destined, nevertheless, to yield nothing more tangible than words. Indiana Governor George N. Craig (1953-1957), increasingly impatient over the federal delays and mindful of progress on the St. Lawrence Seaway scheduled to open in 1959, pushed ahead with plans to finance the project with state funds. Legislation drafted in November 1954 would permit the IBPHT to borrow $3,500,000 from the state's revolving fund to purchase 1,500 acres of land for harbor development. At the same time, a port commission would be established to sell bonds for constructing dock and wharf facilities. The 1955 General Assembly, however, failed to enact the proposed measures. The legislature did authorize the board in 1955 to contract for an economic analysis of the Burns project by an independent firm. Responding quickly to this opportunity, the board hired Harland Bartholomew and Associates of St. Louis to do the study. The firm submitted its report in November 1955, concluding that the proposed port was economically feasible. The report estimated that the total amount of coal and trailership cargo, along with total foreign imports and exports, that would be handled through 1965 would exceed 9,900,000 tons, primarily coal.[17]

Private industrial interests—particularly National Steel, the New York Central Railroad, and the Murchison group, which owned some 1,200 acres of land to the east of National Steel—commissioned their own study of the port's economic feasibility. Conducted by Tippetts-Abbett-McCarthy-Stratton, Engineers of New York and completed in January 1956, this study made more conservative estimates regarding traffic growth by 1965 (expected to reach nearly 6,000,000 tons, again primarily coal), but included an estimate of construction, operation, and debt service expenses. Again, the conclusion was reached that the port would be economically feasible, with annual net revenues and benefits exceeding the debt service charge by $440,000 a year. If, in addition, a steel mill were to be constructed in the area, there could be no question about the port's economic value.[18]

A meeting in March 1956 of interested parties, including National Steel and Corps of Engineers officials, however, failed to secure the desired building commitment from National Steel, but perhaps sparked the interest of a competing firm, Bethlehem Steel. At one time Bethlehem had considered a merger with Youngstown Steel, which had a plant in East Chicago, but the U.S. Department of Justice considered such a merger antithetical to the public interest. Instead, in August 1956, Bethlehem purchased the Murchison group's land and assured the IBPHT that if a public harbor were to be built in the vicinity, the necessary acreage would be available.[19]

By this time, too, both houses of Congress had authorized a general review of all Great Lakes harbors in terms of their readiness for the increased traffic expected following completion of the St. Lawrence Seaway. The Corps of Engineers decided to combine this study with its investigation of the Burns Waterway area, authorized but not funded in 1951. At a large public hearing in Chicago on November 28, 1956, all of the harbors at the southern end of Lake Michigan were discussed. Indiana Governor-elect Harold W. Handley's (1957-1961) strong statement of support for the Burns project overrode local expressions of opposition, and soon thereafter the Corps authorized the preparation of an "interim survey report." Twenty-six years had elapsed since the initial steps leading toward such a report had been taken with the introduction of legislation by Congressman William R. Wood in 1930, but now the day had arrived. Other matters too, comparatively speaking, moved much more rapidly after this time.[20]

In 1957, at the urging of the IBPHT, the Indiana General Assembly appropriated $2,000,000 for use in land acquisitions at the harbor site. The state also sought, without success, updated commitments from the two steel companies about building plants on their properties, something its economic consultants had considered necessary. Nevertheless, the IBPHT proceeded with a new traffic analysis that, for the first time in such studies, considered the impact of a completed St. Lawrence Seaway. Professor Joseph R. Hartley of Indiana University submitted his report in May 1959, which indicated that substantial tonnages in iron ore and grain, and lesser amounts of coal, stone, and general cargo, would yield a total annual savings of some $42,000,000. There were also a number of indirect benefits that would flow from the port, including reduced rates from competing forms of transportation, the likelihood of substantial industrial development in the vicinity, and increased tax revenues to the state.[21]

While the Hartley report was being prepared, the IBPHT also drew up new plans for the design and the precise location of the harbor. The new site, announced in June 1959, was approximately one mile east of the mouth of Burns Waterway, at the point where lands owned by the two steel companies met. Equally important, the design changes provided for a more open harbor that extended into the lake and would allow ample room to expand. The parallel slips leading from the entrance channel in the original plan were replaced with modern docks in a large harbor directly accessible from the lake, obviating in most cases the need for tugboat assistance. These changes would increase the cost of the port somewhat, but would result in a far superior facility. Everything, it appeared, had fallen into place by the end of the 1950s—only a favorable recommendation from the Corps of Engineers was missing, and that arrived in 1960. Instead of calm seas and smooth sailing into the future, however, when the time came to ask the 1961 Indiana General Assembly for the necessary authorizations and appropriations, the port advocates faced a veritable hurricane of opposition, obfuscation, and still more delay.[22]

# CHAPTER 4

# Establishing the Indiana
# Port Commission

While the port project gained momentum during the 1950s, so too did a strong and committed conservation movement. Conservationists in northwest Indiana had one major goal: prevention of further industrialization in the Indiana dunes. This story has been told by two participants in the conservation movement in *Duel for the Dunes: Land Use Conflict on the Shores of Lake Michigan.* The book chronicles the origins of the Save the Dunes Council, Inc., an ongoing conservation group established in 1952 from the ashes of a short-lived Indiana Dunes Preservation Council that had been "solely dedicated to warding off industrialization in the Dunes."[1] The key figure in the Save the Dunes Council was Dorothy Buell, whose life and career is profiled in *Duel for the Dunes.* She was sixty-five years old at the time she organized the council, and she was zealous and indefatigable in her work. By 1956, the organization had 1,000 members and a financial goal of $1,000,000; two years later, it had collected some 500,000 signatures nationwide on a save-the-dunes petition. By that time, Buell also had collected something else that transformed the Save the Dunes Council into a powerful political force: the collaboration of United States Senator Paul H. Douglas of Illinois.

A New Englander and New Yorker by birth and education, Douglas began a teaching career at the University of Chicago in 1920. In 1932, he married Emily Taft, who introduced him to the Indiana dunes. The Douglases built a summer cottage at Ogden Dunes, also the home of Dorothy Buell. Following his legendary voluntary service in the United States Marine Corps during World War II, Douglas was persuaded to switch from an academic to a political career. A liberal Democrat, his success in a race for the United States Senate coincided with Harry S. Truman's (1945-1953) upset victory in the presidential election of 1948. Douglas soon became a powerful force in the country.

According to his autobiography, Douglas had been reluctant to sponsor preservation legislation involving another state, preferring instead that an Indiana senator take the lead in protecting the Indiana dunes. Indiana's senators—William E. Jenner and Homer E. Capehart—however, like many of Indiana's political leaders over the years, were committed to the port project and declined their colleague's overtures. Consequently, on May 26, 1958, Douglas introduced the first of many bills designed to protect the dune lands in Porter County, Indiana, by establishing a national lakeshore there. The bill provided for a 4,000-acre park with a three-and-one-half mile long waterfront; it included the area targeted by the state of Indiana for its port. "It may seem strange," he admitted, "that I should come here from Illinois to plead with all my heart for the protection of a small part of the sovereign State of Indiana . . . . Yet I honestly feel that no apology is necessary, because the issues at stake are of the greatest national significance."[2]

There was an immediate outcry among Indiana journalists, industrialists, and politicians against Douglas: "Together they accused him of unwarranted interference in Indiana's affairs, of representing those Chicago interests that sought to prevent Indiana's industrial development, of carpetbagging, of acting as the 'third Senator from Indiana,' and of wanting a playground outside his own state for blacks and other unwanted Illinois minorities."[3] But Douglas never gave up.

The results of the 1960 election brought Douglas new allies. Included in that category was President John F. Kennedy (1961-1963), who, in addition perhaps to owing his election to Illinois (particularly Chicago) votes, may have seen parallels between the recently established Cape Cod National Seashore (1959) and the Douglas proposals for a national lakeshore on Lake Michigan. Unfortunately for Douglas, however, the elections of 1958 and 1960 also brought Indiana's R. Vance Hartke to the United States Senate and Matthew E. Welsh (1961-1965) to the Indiana governor's office. Both of these men were committed to the idea of a public port for Indiana. An intense battle on the national, state, and local levels raged for several years over the dune lands in northwestern Indiana.

While these battle lines were being drawn, steps leading to the port's formal approval and the beginning of construction were also taking place. Colonel J. A. Smedile, district engineer for the Chicago district of the Corps of Engineers, released his report in October 1960, which favored construction of the Burns Waterway Harbor. The harbor's estimated cost was $34,565,000, a portion of which was expected to come from the federal government for breakwater construction and harbor dredging expenses, customary federal obligations in such undertakings. The benefit-cost ratio of the project was set at a spectacular 5.7 to 1. Moreover, through a recent commitment from Midwest Steel, a subsidiary of National Steel, to begin construction immediately on a finishing mill and, later, to erect a furnace there, the state was able to certify that a fully integrated steel mill would be located adjacent to the port.[4]

Smedile's report had already received the endorsement of the division engineer, but it still needed approval by the chief of engineers, the secretary of the army, and Congress in order to be final. Senator Douglas derailed this approval process in the fall of 1960 by requesting further study of alternate sites. The Corps of Engineers agreed to consider alternate sites, even though its own findings in 1944 indicated that there were no other suitable sites. This move also ignored an act of the Indiana legislature in 1959 that excluded counties with three or more second-class cities (that is, Lake County) from having a port authority. Furthermore, the state, when it established the Indiana Port Commission in 1961, prohibited selection of any existing harbor as the port project site, again eliminating the Lake County alternatives favored by Douglas and others.[5]

A major step forward had been made, of course, with the establishment of the Indiana Port Commission in 1961. Governor Welsh had not focused on the port issue during his campaign in the fall of 1960. When he spoke of Indiana's transportation needs at that time, he gave priority to highways and Ohio River bridges. He was, however, committed to the state's economic development and made the port issue a priority item during his entire four years in office, even sharing his "cordial . . . no-nonsense" administrative assistant, Clinton Green, with the Port Commission for two years. Green, a civil engineer with, in the governor's words, "a flair for administration and a passion for detail," served as the first secretary-treasurer of the Port Commission from April 1961 until he resigned in February 1964 to campaign for the Democratic nomination for governor.[6]

The bill establishing the Indiana Port Commission sailed through both houses of the legislature and was signed into law by the governor on March 2, 1961. Only four dissenting votes—including three from disappointed Lake County representatives—were cast against it. According to the law, the Port Commission's purpose was promotion of "the agricultural, industrial and commercial development of the state," and its charge was construction, "in cooperation with the federal government, or otherwise, of a modern port." The commission was instructed to pay "particular attention to the benefits which may accrue to the state and its citizens from the St. Lawrence Seaway." The commission was to have "five (5) members, appointed by the governor, no more than three (3) of whom shall be members of the same political party." Members were to have staggered four-year terms of office and receive (once the governor certified that the port was functioning) an annual salary.[7]

The extensive powers and responsibilities of the commission were spelled out in the thirty-section act. It had the power of eminent domain for obtaining the necessary land, including land under water and riparian rights. Unlike the Indiana Board of Public Harbors and Terminals (IBPHT) that it replaced, the Port Commission was authorized "to issue port revenue bonds of the state payable solely from revenues" to finance the project: land acquisition, engineering, construction, legal expenses, and more. It had the obligation, once expenses had been met and the revenue bonds redeemed, to pay "all surplus net revenues thereafter derived from the operation of such port into the state general fund." The law also required annual reports, a journal of all "final actions," and annual audits by the Indiana State Board of Accounts. No major appropriations to the Port Commission were made at this time, but monies previously available to the IBPHT were transferred to the commission. The transfer included the $2,000,000 appropriated in 1957 for land acquisition purposes.[8]

After the law was enacted, Governor Welsh moved quickly to appoint commission members and get their work underway. His first choices were James R. Fleming, owner and publisher of the Fort Wayne *Journal-Gazette*; Robert M. Schram, a Peru farmer and banker; Albert L. Yeager, a businessman from Michigan City; William E. Shumaker, a prominent industrialist from Indianapolis; and George A. Nelson, who, after leaving the Valparaiso Chamber of Commerce, had been employed as director of personnel at the Continental Diamond Fibre Company there. All of these men were sworn into office at the first meeting of the commission held on April 10, 1961 in Porter County at the Spa Restaurant outside the town of Porter. The day's ceremonies began with a morning tour of the eventual port site, a spot still difficult to reach without four-wheel-drive vehicles and local guides. Administration of the oaths of office and brief talks by Professor Joseph Hartley of Indiana University and Colonel Smedile of the Corps of Engineers followed. After lunch, Governor Welsh delivered brief remarks, pledging full support from his office and the state's commitment to the project. He used the occasion to make the point that Indiana was determined to have the port. If the federal government did not fulfill its responsibility by sharing in the construction costs, as had

Robert M. Schram served as an Indiana Port Commission commissioner, 1961-1983, and chairman, 1969.

been customary for similar projects around the country, "Indiana will undertake the entire job itself." In an obvious jab at Senator Douglas of Illinois, Welsh asserted that "We will not permit the commercial and industrial growth of our state . . . to be thwarted by the unfortunate and unwise delaying tactics of those whose primary responsibility is to other areas of our nations [*sic*]."[9]

Governor Welsh then presided over the election of a commission chairman, James R. Fleming, who conducted the remainder of the first Port Commission meeting. Several important steps were taken at that meeting. Recognizing the need for an early test of the constitutionality of the Port Commission law, attorneys John E. Hurt (of McNutt, Hurt, and Blue, Martinsville) and John I. Bradshaw, Jr. (of McHale, Cook, Welch and McKinney, Indianapolis) were retained to represent the Port Commission on "the possibility of litigation on testing the constitutionality of the Act." Additionally, the Port Commission retained Harry T. Ice, an Indianapolis attorney who specialized in revenue bond issues, as its bond counselor. Most significantly, the board set May 3, 1961 for a public hearing in the Indiana State House regarding selection of a site for the port.[10]

Dunes advocates claimed that the hearing was a charade, citing as evidence preliminary land agreements between the state and the

Bethlehem Steel Company that related to the Burns site. The formal hearing was, however, a necessary legal step. According to the Port Commission meeting minutes for May 3, "a notice of public hearing . . . was duly published in every daily newspaper in the State of Indiana," announcing the meeting and the Port Commission's eagerness to hear opinions in reference to the port's "location and general economic effect." Groups and individuals desiring to be heard were asked to limit their oral presentations to five minutes, and to submit written copies of their statements for the record.[11]

Chairman Fleming presided throughout the day-long event, listening to some sixty-four statements of support and opposition. Three former governors were among those who supported locating the port in the Burns Waterway area; former Governor Harold W. Handley (1957-1961) was most conversant and outspoken about the matter. He called the Burns area virgin territory conducive to new economic growth and new jobs for the state and admonished the commission to "do it quickly."

Professor Joseph Hartley of Indiana University also spoke. He recalled the economic analysis he had done for the IBPHT in 1958 and placed some of its findings into the record. The traffic potential at Burns, he believed, was enormous; moreover, another virtue of the site was the land available for "back-up facilities." Representatives from both Bethlehem Steel and Midwest Steel also submitted statements; they again expressed their willingness to cooperate with the state in building a public port and their intention to build a private port for their own use if necessary. "We couldn't use a public port anywhere else," stated John Laughlin of Midwest Steel.

The South Bend and South Shore Railroad Company representative gave figures indicating sizable mutual benefits to the port and the railroad; a New York Central Railroad Company spokesman pointed out that good highways, utilities, and railroads were already in place at Burns. Enos Coal Company's representative Arthur Scales agreed that a public harbor was vital to the economy of the state. He suggested, however, that the previous speakers had missed the point and asserted that there would be a harbor at Burns: "the question is whether it will be open to all, or not." He also underscored the need for a large amount of land in the port area to handle, for example, fifteen thousand carloads of coal.

Speakers in opposition to Burns Harbor included some mayors and chambers of commerce in Lake County, who ignored the legislative restrictions and revived the idea of a Tri-City port in the East

Chicago-Whiting-Hammond area; the Gary Chamber of Commerce, unlike the mayor of Gary, supported the Burns Waterway site. More persuasive in their opposition were the most prominent leaders of the Save the Dunes Council—Dorothy Buell, Thomas E. Dustin, Herbert Read—and several individuals from northwestern Indiana. Buell emphasized that the council was not a "fly-by-night organization" or a group of "birdwatchers" and was not against industry per se: "We are conservationists like Theodore Roosevelt and Carl Sandburg and we favor both a port and a park." The port, however, she believed, should be in already industrialized Lake County. She also summarized the history of the Save the Dunes Council and the association of Senator Douglas with it, and defended his motives regarding preservation of the dunes.

For the most part, Fleming indulged all of the witnesses, occasionally engaging in some light banter or offering corrections to obvious misstatements of fact. Interestingly, Captain Ola F. Heslar, the last chairman of the IBPHT, was there to offer his view on the controversial point of whether the Corps of Engineers had ever surveyed Indiana's entire Lake Michigan shoreline. He believed that it had and quoted the 1949 engineering report to that effect. Significantly, too, the Michigan City representatives spoke of recent changes in their attitudes and expressed their new-found support for the Burns Waterway site. Civic and labor organizations in Portage—a town destined, in Fleming's view, to become a model city of perhaps 100,000 people—favored the port's location within its town limits.

The Republican Women's Club, for example, favored the port, and one of its members read a Gary *Post-Tribune* editorial of May 2, 1961—"Time to Pick a Site"—into the record. There were "major drawbacks" to the Tri-City site, particularly the lack of room for new industry, whereas the Burns Waterway site would not only serve the steel companies already there but attract many new industries in the future. "This represents our views," concluded the clubwoman, "and those of ninety-nine percent of the people of Portage." Toward the end of the hearing, state Senator Earl Landgrebe, a former opponent of the port who was converted to the project by George Nelson during the 1961 session of the General Assembly, made the new and telling point that the legislative intent, both in 1957 and 1961, was to build a port in the Burns Waterway area.

As the hearing indicated, and as increasingly strident views in the newspapers of Indiana and neighboring states reinforced, the two sides in the "port or park" fight were far apart. As more and more pieces in the complex jigsaw puzzle, which seemed to picture a modern port at Burns Waterway, fell into place, the differences increased and the feelings intensified. Conservationists and port advocates continued on parallel courses that would meet—or collide—eventually.

Matters on the port side moved forward rapidly in 1961. On May 18, during a meeting of the Port Commission in Chicago, the board formally selected a port site in the Burns Waterway area.[12] Shortly after that, on the national level, Senator Hartke introduced a compromise national lakeshore bill; it provided for both a park, as Senator Douglas wanted, and a port, as state leaders in Indiana wanted, along the Indiana shore of Lake Michigan. The Hartke bill provided for a contiguous national park, adjacent to (and at one time even including) the Indiana Dunes State Park. The Douglas bill had reserved five divided parcels of land, including Bethlehem Steel Company and Burns Harbor port expansion lands, but not the Ogden Dunes area, the location of some of the finest dunelands in Indiana as well as numerous expensive homes.[13]

The news on the legal front was also encouraging. The lawsuit (*Orbison* v. *Welsh*) intended to establish the validity of the Port Commission's enabling statute was filed in the Superior Court of Marion County in May. On June 30, 1961, the local judge ruled that the Port Commission act was constitutional, but the case needed to be appealed up the line in order to get a definitive ruling. With the approval of the Indiana Court of Appeals, the matter went directly to the Indiana Supreme Court in September. In January 1962, Judge Frederick Landis, Jr. spoke for a unanimous court in upholding the constitutionality of the Port Commission act in all particulars.[14] At the same time, other courts were invalidating various Save the Dunes Council challenges to the Port Commission's powers. Such litigation was one of the major tactics the council elected to use in battling the port.[15]

While the legal mills were turning, the additional steps required to obtain Corps of Engineers approval also took place. On August 30, 1961, again at the State House in Indianapolis, the Chicago district engineer, Colonel J. A. Smedile, conducted another large public hearing on the port. His report of the previous year had been returned for additional information, and the purpose of the hearing in August was to elicit the latest facts and figures available that would impinge upon the issue of the port's economic viability. Governor Welsh did his part in publicizing the meeting and encouraging participation. He distributed a four-page information sheet containing a letter, map, and historical review. His letter emphasized that the Port Commission would "be promoting the agricultural, industrial, and commercial development of the State." Plans were made for him to write to legislators and enclose a certification-of-support form and a petition to circulate for signatures. According to a story in the Indianapolis *Star,* August 30, 1961, "An avalanche of testimony favorable to the Port of Indiana at Burns Ditch" was received for the hearing. That testimony was to be augmented by statements from political leaders, past and present, Democratic and Republican.[16]

Several hundred people, supporters as well as opponents, occupied the House of Representatives chamber or the hall outside, where the House loudspeaker system had been turned on. Colonel Smedile permitted a more open-ended and vigorous discussion of the issues than had Chairman Fleming three months earlier. Witnesses were allowed to speak "as long and as loudly as they wished, frequently to applause and often to boos." The meeting lasted from 10 a.m. until late in the evening, with more than 100 speakers. Mayor Walter M. Jeorse of East Chicago, "in a loud and fiery speech," called again for a Lake County port and assailed Indiana's current and former governors, and its congressional delegation. He proposed an eleventh commandment for them: "Thou shalt not commit silly, idiotic nincompoopery." He called the identical bills, which were introduced in the United States House and Senate to create a smaller national park than the one Senator Douglas had proposed, a "smokescreen of confusion." Finally, he voiced his fears of an eventual "asphalt jungle and an island of smokestacks" in Porter County.[17]

Jeorse and his colleagues were answered, primarily, by Clinton Green, who presented the state's major testimony. He submitted "a mass of resolutions and petitions from trade associations, chambers of commerce, farm organizations, legislators and labor unions containing thousands of names." He also presented all of the letters of protest received—twelve in number, including one from Michigan. Many other state officials made brief statements of support.[18]

Former Governor Handley not only testified at the August hearing, but he also weighed into the battle in an even more significant fashion with an article published in a trade publication, *Indiana Business and Industry,* in September. His answer to the question of the necessity for a port in Indiana stressed national security considerations (similar factors had tipped the balance in favor of a comprehensive interstate highway program a few years earlier) and state economic development factors—the port of Indiana offered great opportunities for industrial expansion. As a "convenient port of entry, in the heart

The Calumet River, part of the Port of Chicago, in 1961 showing the congestion of bridges and river bends; aerial view looking northeast.

of the nation's Midwest, for the commerce of the world," the project would yield thousands of new jobs for the state. Moreover, the Burns Harbor site offered special advantages—economy in construction, access to major markets, and favorable hydrographic conditions.[19]

Handley also provided a brief historical review of the port project since 1937, pointing out that before completion of the St. Lawrence Seaway the smaller harbors in the state at East Chicago and Michigan City were adequate, but now there was a new demand for modern facilities. He recognized that the two steel companies near the Burns site were "the most important single factor in the justification of the project," but he stressed that "The steel companies *do not need* the public port." However necessary the steel tonnage would be to the "public port, the reverse is not true! . . . these companies can well afford to construct their own private docks or harbors." He concluded that the state was building "A public port to serve the entire Midwest—not a port for the steel mills, but a public port *because* of the steel mills." The Port Commission had extra copies of Governor Handley's article printed and distributed them widely.[20]

Colonel Smedile, in February 1962, submitted a report to his superiors in Washington recommending that construction on the Burns Waterway Harbor project be authorized. His conclusion, based upon new data and revised plans for the proposed harbor was that the project was economically feasible. These plans reduced anticipated federal expenditures for harbor preparations from $34,500,000 to $25,500,000. In a very short time, on March 23, 1962, the Board of Engineers for Rivers and Harbors concurred with Smedile. Now the issue was before Congress and the executive branch as a policy—not an engineering or economic—matter. An important milestone had been reached, but the end was not yet in sight.[21]

An aerial view of the Calumet Region, circa 1964; lines at upper center show proposed location of Burns Harbor.

# CHAPTER 5

# Funding and Construction on Lake Michigan

During the early 1960s, the Indiana Port Commission attempted to persuade the federal government to embrace and offer federal funding for its customary portion of the port construction project. Clinton Green became a familiar figure in Washington as he moved between 1600 Pennsylvania Avenue and Capitol Hill to conduct his lobbying activities. He attended Senate committee hearings on the Paul H. Douglas and R. Vance Hartke national lakeshore park bills in February 1962, which led to another round of arguments regarding the merits of the port project. Senator Douglas repeated his intention, if the park bill failed, to "fight them to the death on the harbor appropriation." In addition to his concerns about increased pollution, he said the park was "needed for recreation by the 7,000,000 urban dwellers in the expanding metropolitan complex from Gary to Milwaukee." The need to save the dunes, he concluded, "had become a regional and national concern rather than purely a state matter."[1]

Instead of engaging in public debate at that time, Green focused on getting Bureau of the Budget and executive branch approval of the U.S. Army Corps of Engineers' recommendations. On July 5, he accompanied Governor Matthew E. Welsh (1961-1965) to the White House, where they met with President John F. Kennedy (1961-1963) and several advisers. At a news conference later that day, a reporter

# A Rude Awakening!

Credit: Charles G. Werner, artist, and Indianapolis *Star.*

Cartoon, circa 1962, depicting Illinois' U.S. Senator Paul H. Douglas "burying" Indiana Governor Matthew E. Welsh and Indiana's U.S. Senator R. Vance Hartke and their plans for a Lake Michigan port.

asked President Kennedy if he gave Governor Welsh "any encouragement." Kennedy replied, "No . . . . The Budget Bureau is having an analysis made tomorrow which Governor Welsh and his representatives will attend. There will also be a White House representative there . . . we will make a report or recommendation to the Congress shortly."[2]

On October 3, however, Indiana's hopes for immediate federal support were dashed when the 1962 rivers and harbors act was passed by the House of Representatives without an appropriation for an Indiana port. The omission of port support from the bill led to unusually harsh rhetoric from two normally reserved men. Republican Lieutenant Governor Richard O. Ristine (1961-1965) charged that Kennedy's actions were punishment for Kennedy's loss in Indiana and a payback to the Chicago politicians for his thin electoral margin in 1960. Democratic Governor Welsh, only a bit more circumspect, vowed that the state would go ahead with the project, and "seek federal reimbursement later." Welsh said the expected endorsement from the Bureau of the Budget did not get issued in time to affect the bill because of "blackmail" by Senator Douglas.[3]

In the meantime, the debate within Indiana and the adjacent state of Illinois escalated. The Save the Dunes Council called for a massive letter-writing campaign to U.S. senators and representatives, urging approval of the Douglas park bill (which would kill the port project) rather than the Hartke bill (which would let both projects proceed). The Chicago *Tribune* weighed in with a heavy editorial barrage against the port, as did Len O'Connor, a respected newsman who aired a nightly commentary on the NBC-TV affiliate in Chicago.[4] Writers for the Louisville *Courier-Journal,* the New York *Times,* and the *Christian Science Monitor* supported the conservationist position, ignoring, downplaying, or misstating the position of port proponents.

On October 29, 1962, however, Special Counsel Lee C. White wrote to Governor Welsh that the Bureau of the Budget report would probably be favorable. The Congress could then debate the policy issues. White noted that President Kennedy's desire was "that both a deep port and a national lakeshore area . . . can be developed."[5]

There was a mild flurry within the Port Commission on May 16, 1962. Ignoring the fact that reporters were present prior to the Port Commission meeting, Attorney General Edwin Steers demanded clarification of the question of legal representation—whether he and his office or private counsel should handle the commission's land purchases. The commission went into executive session as Steers reportedly stormed out. Chairman James R. Fleming accepted responsibility for the problem—in his view a misunderstanding only—after which the commission reiterated its position that "the Commission should spend no more on legal services than necessary," and that the attorney general's office would provide most legal services. Steers then allowed a land transaction with National Steel (acting on behalf of its subsidiary, Midwest Steel) to proceed after his staff had reviewed it.[6]

The 1963 Indiana General Assembly session held great promise for the Port Commission. In his message to the General Assembly on January 11, Governor Welsh proposed establishment of a Fund for Economic Development to help "do those things, engage in those activities and invest that money—public and private, that we know will produce for us the immediate or eventual expansion of our industry, our business, our farm markets and our number of jobs." The fund proposal included "construction of the outer breakwater of the Port of Indiana." Welsh, in his address, clearly stated the position and rationale of the port's proponents:

> With the rapid development of the European Common Market and the need for opening additional foreign as well as domestic markets for Indiana industrial and agricultural products, the construction of the Port of Indiana offers one of our finest opportunities for improving the economy of the state. Yet, again if we must wait until Federal funds are available for the construction of the key outer breakwater for the port, we may miss forever our opportunity to build an active public port serving the business and agriculture of Indiana.
>
> I emphasize public port, for there is no doubt but that either a private or a public port will be built at Burns Waterway. Both the Midwest and Bethlehem Steel Companies have indicated that their plans for development of their land on the shores of Lake Michigan require port facilities. The question is, will the port be constructed by two steel companies for their exclusive and private use, or will there be a public deep water port benefitting the entire state.[7]

The economic development proposal was a complex package of projects "designed to appeal to different interests and different areas of the state, and to create the broad-based support . . . needed for legislative passage," Welsh noted in a later assessment. Inclusion of a Porter County port in the package, however, ultimately would have doomed the package to failure: "Our principal and very active opposition came from the Lake County steel interests," wrote Welsh. Lake County Democrats, he asserted, "felt their job was to protect the large steel industries of Lake County from the competition that construction of a port would bring."[8]

It required a special session of the General Assembly, convened immediately following the 1963 regular session, to achieve needed financial reforms for the state and a state budget. In last-minute negotiating, Welsh was able to shepherd economic development proposals through the General Assembly—paid for with an increase in cigarette taxes; construction funds for the port were not included. The legislature, however, authorized Port Commission expenditure of up to $600,000, "from existing appropriations," to permit engineering, design, and financial studies to continue. The 1963 legislature also amended the Port Commission enabling statute, broadening its powers to include construction and operation of an Ohio River port in Vanderburgh County.[9]

Although disappointed at the failure to get full funding, release of some of the previously appropriated money was enough to activate the Port Commission. It had already identified and entered into preliminary discussions with an engineering and consulting firm of some prominence—Sverdrup & Parcel and Associates, Inc. of St. Louis. This firm had worked for the state of Indiana previously, and Clinton Green recommended that the Port Commission approach the firm. After some initial contacts, the commission received a proposal by Sverdrup & Parcel to plan and design its deepwater port on Lake Michigan. On July 3, 1963, on a plane en route to a meeting in St. Louis with officers of Sverdrup & Parcel, the commission decided that a final draft of the proposal from Sverdrup & Parcel would be considered by the commission at its regular July meeting. The final agreement was signed July 11 after action by the commission.[10]

Sverdrup & Parcel worked rapidly. The firm provided its *Burns Waterway Harbor Interim Report* in January 1964. Informed by the insights of other specialists hired by Sverdrup & Parcel as well as by a "model study" of the Burns Harbor configuration, undertaken by hydrologists at the University of Florida, the report laid out the specifications for a completely modern port[11]—the first port on Lake Michigan designed according to St. Lawrence Seaway specifications.[12]

The 117-page *Interim Report*—sixty-four narrative pages and fifty-three plates—describes an inverted U-shaped port, with the outer harbor protected by a giant breakwater nearly a mile long that angled northeastward into Lake Michigan. Between the point of the breakwater and the east harbor wall, a 400-foot-wide entrance permitted ships to enter a twenty-seven-foot-deep harbor without tugboat assistance. The largest and deepest-draft ships on the Great Lakes, or those able to get there via the St. Lawrence Seaway, could easily be accommodated at Burns Harbor. They would dock at an area between the two arms of the harbor comprised of landfill and extending lakeward beyond the original shoreline. The landfill area would add approximately ninety-five acres to the size of the port and would provide a place to deposit materials dredged from the harbor site. Clinton Green, secretary-treasurer of the Port Commission, summed up the situation: "we are getting 95 additional acres with an outer harbor that costs $8,500,000 less."

The total estimated cost of stage one of the project—which included general cargo and special terminal facilities as well as a port railroad—was $92,470,000, of which $16,090,000 (for breakwater construction and approach channel dredging) was eligible for federal reimbursement. Most importantly, the study indicated that the port project was economically feasible, with good road and rail connections already in place. Other developments added dramatically to the port's economic potential: the 1959 completion of the St. Lawrence Seaway and industrial development in northwestern Indiana, particularly the Midwest Steel and Bethlehem Steel mill sites immediately adjacent to the port. According to the economic analysis, the so-called harbor service or economic impact area of the port, based upon an evaluation of existing rail and truck lines, extended westward all the way to the Wyoming coal fields. There would be an impact, by rail or truck or both, on as many as twelve states. Additionally, properly licensed Ohio and Mississippi river barges entering Lake Michigan via the Calumet River could call at the port. Finally, the report mentioned plans of the New York Central Railroad Company to build a 4,100-car classification yard at the port site.

An eighteen-page economic feasibility section of the study carefully analyzed the economies of the 588 counties within the twelve-state tributary area, examining their total industrial and agricultural production and existing transportation methods and costs. The report concluded: "The public port at Burns Harbor will make its greatest contribution . . . if it provides facilities designed to repatriate traffic already generated but moving through coastal ports; facilities designed to serve available traffic not now moving; and facilities designed to replace existing facilities which are inadequate in themselves, or lack efficient water access for modern deep-water vessels."

The report cited two new areas of potential profit: a refrigerated warehouse for frozen meat and a refinery for raw sugar. Most prominent in the report's "inadequate existing facilities category" was coal. It was noted that the Port of Chicago was handicapped by terminals which were difficult and time-consuming to reach and therefore expensive. Coal rates from Chicago to other Great Lakes ports carried an increase of twelve cents per ton because to reach its major coal transfer facility "a lake or ocean vessel must traverse a stretch of the Calumet River which includes seven highway and railroad bridges."

The author of this section of the report, James C. Buckley, estimated that as much as 7,700,000 to 11,700,000 tons of traffic were available "to a public port at Burns Harbor" in 1968, with 14,700,000 to 18,700,000 tons available by 1985. He warned, however, that the Port Commission's task in operating the port would be more than just "day-to-day housekeeping." There would have to be "a strong program of port protection whose objective will be the maintenance of fair, equitable, and non-descriminatory [*sic*] inland and ocean rates, and a strong program of port promotion whose objectives will be the development and maintenance of needed services." The report also noted that Burns Harbor would be expected to benefit from foreign trade "currently using coastal ports." Space had been allowed in the port plan for future use as a foreign trade zone.

Burns Waterway Harbor under initial construction in 1965; aerial view looking south from Lake Michigan.

The Port Commission's investment in development, the report proposed, would create a variety of revenue sources: harbor dues, "assessed on the basis of the net register tonnage of the vessel" using the harbor; dockage and wharfage charges, the former a vessel tie-up fee and the latter a cargo-based fee; ground and facility rental charges, including office space within the administration building or other commercial buildings erected at the port; and fees for using various port terminal utilities supplied by the commission.

Armed with Sverdrup & Parcel's extensive *Interim Report*, the Port Commission looked forward to the 1965 session of the General Assembly. Lafayette attorney Roger D. Branigin won the Democratic gubernatorial nomination in the spring of 1964 and, in the fall, was elected governor. Fortunately for port advocates, Branigin (1965-1969) was as committed as Welsh to the state's economic development, and to the Lake Michigan port. According to his final address to the General Assembly on January 8, 1965, Welsh considered the "public port on Lake Michigan" his "largest, single piece of unfinished business" upon leaving office. In that address, he reviewed for the legislature the port's progress since 1961, and pointed with pride to the "great steel processing complexes [that] have grown up on each side of the harbor site." The Midwest Steel rolling mill was already in operation, employing 1,300 people; and 4,800 construction workers were busy on an integrated plant for Bethlehem Steel with a total investment of $350,000,000. Port construction had not followed suit because of "long and frustrating delays" in Congress. Welsh indicated that the Port Commission request to the State Budget Committee had been cut in the final budget before the legislature. He asked legislators to ignore the State Budget Committee's recommendation and restore the budget bill to the full amount—$25,570,000—of the Port Commission's original request: "This action would permit the Port Commission to move ahead immediately."[13]

In his first message to the General Assembly, delivered just four days later, Governor Branigin fully embraced Welsh's approach: "The early completion of a public harbor on Lake Michigan is the single greatest contribution which we can make to an expanding economy. An appropriation of $25,000,000 to this project will be a giant step toward the future. This is a large sum of money, I know. But the experts who have studied the problem tell us that the investment will be returned to us many times over. It is an investment in the future which we cannot fail to make."[14]

Such high-level pleadings, reinforced by the Port Commission's own lobbying efforts, resulted in a compromise solution—$15,000,000 was appropriated in the 1965 regular appropriations bill. An additional $10,570,000 was appropriated over the next two years from cigarette tax revenues. The Port Commission was instructed to repay the cigarette tax money to the state general fund "at the earliest practicable time" from port revenues. Neither of these appropriations, however, would have to be repaid if the federal government did not make its anticipated reimbursement.[15] The General Assembly also passed legislation enabling the Port Commission to apply to the federal government to establish foreign trade zones in Indiana and giving the commission power of eminent domain for the acquisition of property.[16]

Attention focused again on the national level. Not only did the state want Congress to adopt a bill authorizing federal reimbursement for the port project, but it also needed a license from the U.S. Army Corps of Engineers to permit construction to begin. Senator Paul Douglas, still pushing for a national park at the port site, amended the authorization bill so that no federal funds would be forthcoming until after the Indiana Dunes National Lakeshore had been authorized. In the meantime, Douglas was expected "to obstruct approval of the license by the Army engineers."[17]

While this showdown in the U.S. Senate between Douglas and Indiana senators Birch E. Bayh and R. Vance Hartke was developing, the U.S. House of Representatives prepared to consider the dunes park bill, already passed by the Senate, and related legislation. Indiana Representative J. Edward Roush had sought a hearing on the dunes bill with the House interior committee. Indiana Representative Charles A. Halleck was a member of the public works committee, which would hear testimony regarding the port bill. The Indiana delegation in Washington expected resolution of the port-park question during 1965, but it looked for "an intense legislative battle on both measures before they are sent to the President."[18]

The final version of the rivers and harbors bill, which included the Burns Waterway Harbor, was agreed to by a House-Senate conference committee on October 18, passed by both houses of Congress, and signed by President Lyndon B. Johnson (1963-1969) on October 27, 1965. It authorized up to $25,000,000 in reimbursement payments to the state of Indiana, subject to satisfactory assurances "to the Secretary of the Army that water and air pollution sources will be controlled to the maximum extent feasible in order to minimize any adverse effects on public recreational areas in the general vicinity of the Har-

Credit: Valparaiso Vidette-Messenger, October 2, 1968.

Commemoration of the completion of the outer breakwaters at Burns
Harbor in 1968.

bor. No appropriation is authorized to be made for the construction of
this project until the Indiana Dunes National Lakeshore has been
voted upon by both Houses of Congress during the same Congress."
Construction had to begin within three years of the enactment of the
law, or the reimbursement authorization would expire.[19]

Although a few preliminary construction steps had already been
taken, such as aerial surveys and test borings, both on and offshore,
the first construction contract for building Burns Harbor was let in
November 1965 to the Walsh Construction Company of Gary. The
$136,920 contract was for grading the site and building a temporary
access road for harbor construction crews. A contract for the initial
track of the Port Terminal Railroad was awarded in December to the
Railroad Construction Company of Ashtabula, Ohio. After receipt of
Corps of Engineers' conditional approval in May 1966 of Sverdrup &
Parcel's design memorandum, based on its 1964 *Interim Report,* the
Port Commission solicited bids for major construction. On June 9,
1966, a contract in the amount of $10,162,210 was awarded to Peter
Kiewet and Sons of Omaha, Nebraska to begin construction of the

north breakwater, west outer bulkhead, and east inner bulkhead. The Port Commission negotiated several other contracts in this period. It also obtained special "wrap-up" insurance with broad liability coverage for the commission and its contractors.[20]

An elaborate celebration for formal groundbreaking was held on October 10, 1966. Clinton Green and George A. Nelson, the Port Commission's chief actors over the years, were in charge of arrangements and presided at the festivities. The crowd of approximately 650 people who came to Burns Harbor that day included dignitaries from industry, labor, and all levels of government. Winds estimated at forty to fifty miles per hour caused problems during the program. Master of Ceremonies Nelson interrupted Senator Birch Bayh just as he began to speak, asking the audience to move because the tent they were in was about to be blown away. When he resumed, Senator Bayh remarked "that the wind was significant because there had been so much about the project." More seriously, "he said that the project was important because of the jobs it would mean to the state." Governor Branigin reflected upon the state's thirty-five-year struggle for the port, and what it would mean in the future for the state's economy. He also complimented Midwest Steel and Bethlehem Steel for their roles in the project, and thanked the New York Central Railroad for building its classification yard there. The governor then gave the signal for the USS *Portage* to fire a salute to the occasion, but the wind prevented the noise of the three-inch gun from reaching land. The crowd witnessed puffs of smoke repeatedly, marking what the governor called "the quietest shots he had [ever] seen."[21]

Others who spoke during the proceedings were Port Commission Chairman James R. Fleming, who particularly praised Indiana governors Handley, Welsh, and Branigin for their unswerving support. Congressman Charles A. Halleck, who had dedicated years to this project in his district, appropriately made the most extensive remarks of the day. He reviewed the major events since the 1930s leading to the port, suggesting that congressional approval would have come "in 1962 except for certain roadblocks which perhaps I have already mentioned enough times"—meaning, of course, the work of Senator Douglas to get a national park established in Porter County. Halleck noted that he had to leave immediately following the dedication in order to return to Washington to vote on the park bill the following day. The result of this vote allowed the port and the national park projects to proceed.[22]

Port Commissioner Robert M. Schram has indicated that on his early visits to the port site he had found it difficult to visualize a port

The SS *Lehigh* entering Burns Waterway Harbor on September 11, 1969. It was the first domestic ship to use Burns Waterway Harbor and delivered a load of iron ore for Bethlehem Steel.

on the windswept, rugged terrain of the lakeshore between two large steel mills. Many visitors to the site that day probably had similar problems, but within a matter of months a port began to emerge from amid the construction activity.

Soon the outline of the harbor was visible, the result of moving enormous amounts of sand, stone, and spoil material. The north, or outer, breakwater stretched 4,600 feet across the top of the project, and a similar rubble-stone extension from the west dockwall linked with it several hundred feet from shore. Although the outer breakwater extended only fourteen feet above lake level, and was fifty-five feet wide at that point, it was 200 feet wide at its base located several feet below the lake bottom. It contained successive layers of sand, core stone, and stone, with increasingly larger limestone blocks at the top, randomly placed in order to break up the waves more readily and

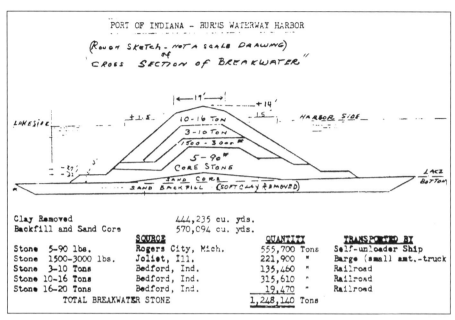

Rough sketch of cross section of breakwater at Burns Harbor, circa 1960s.

weighing from sixteen to twenty tons each. The average lake depth at the breakwater site was forty feet.[23]

Even the Kiewet company, accustomed to huge multi-million dollar projects, seemed impressed by the magnitude of the Burns Harbor undertaking. An issue of *Kie-Ways*, a company publication, carried a cover picture of the last stone being placed on the breakwater. An accompanying article described the project, and the methods used in placing the stone. The core stone had been shipped in self-unloading vessels on loan from the United States Steel Corporation, and "was dumped in place by the vessels and dressed to grade by a barge-mounted dragline." The large outer stones were placed by a dragline on a special barge. Completion of this phase of construction, celebrated on October 1, 1968, with placement "of 'the final stone,'" was witnessed by Sverdrup & Parcel representatives, officers from the U.S. Army Corps of Engineers, and members of the Indiana Port Commission.[24]

The Port Commission's annual report for 1969 was very positive. Construction activities had gone well, except for a work stoppage from April to September 1969 by workers for the dredging contractor. This had not prevented use of the harbor—for the first time—by a Bethle-

Indiana Port Commission commissioners in June 1969 were (from left)
Henry R. Sackett; Robert M. Schram, vice chairman; Joseph N. Thomas,
chairman; William E. Shumaker, secretary-treasurer; and George A. Nelson.

hem Steel Corporation oreboat, the SS *Lehigh,* on September 11,
1969. "Bethlehem Steel's Burns Harbor plant produced its first steel"
on December 17.[25]

Believing, along with other commission members, "that the construction of the deep water port is virtually complete," James R. Fleming, the elderly chairman of the Port Commission, announced his
retirement in April 1969. Robert Schram, vice chairman of the commission since its inception, was elected as his successor. In June,
Republican Governor Edgar D. Whitcomb (1969-1973) named attorney Joseph N. Thomas, Gary, to the Port Commission. According to
Schram, the governor preferred to have a man of his own party as
chairman, and Schram nominated Thomas to be the chairman.
Thomas, a Republican, was then elected chairman, and Schram, a
Democrat, was elected vice chairman. Thomas was only the second
newcomer on the commission during its first nine years. Michigan
City industrialist Albert L. Yeager had resigned after serving three
years, and Henry R. Sackett of Gary had replaced him.

An equally important change in port administration came with the
appointment of a port director in September 1969. At Governor Whitcomb's request, the commission appointed a three-person search
committee—Chairman Thomas, Nelson, and state Senator John Van
Ness. Their choice—Jack P. Fitzgerald of Tampa, Florida—had seventeen years of experience at the Port of Tampa, and he came highly recommended.[26]

In addition to a port director, the commission also obtained its first port tenant in 1969. In October, the Levy Corporation of Detroit leased a ten-acre tract in order to build a slag processing operation, utilizing an abundant waste product from the nearby steel mills. Its plant costs of $430,000 were to be met through a bond issue, with lessee payments retiring the bonds. In addition, the company "guaranteed payment of standard dockage and wharfage fees ranging from $3,000.00 to $10,000.00 annually during the life of the lease."

The commission received a total of almost $870,869 in refunds from insurance companies "because claims and losses were far less than anticipated" under the "wrap-up" coverage in the early construction phase. In addition, Chairman Thomas and Governor Whitcomb executed the federal reimbursement agreement for a partial payment of $10,311,651.

Work toward an Ohio River port was also begun with the appropriation of $50,000 for a Feasibility Study of the Posey-Vanderburgh Area.[27] According to the 1969 *Annual Report,* "discussions were held with interested groups from Evansville and Mt. Vernon, two cities in the proposed area. Plans were made for the Feasibility Study to get underway early next year, and Lieutenant Governor Richard E. Folz (1969-1973) appointed a five-man Regional Advisory Committee to work with the Port Commission for the early development of a river port."

Thomas and Fitzgerald introduced the 1969 *Annual Report,* calling 1969 "A Year of Transition," and indicating their optimism for 1970: "We intend to step up the pace of development during 1970. The grand opening celebration tentatively scheduled for July of 1970 should be the highlight of the year. This opening celebration should bring to the attention of everyone the vast potential that exists for national and international trade and commerce in our wonderful State of Indiana."

Burns Waterway Harbor; aerial view looking northeast.

Credit: *Indiana Business and Industry,* September 1970.

## CHAPTER 6

# Getting Started:
# The First Decade of Operations

One can only imagine George Nelson's emotions as he participated in the official dedication of the Port of Indiana at Burns Harbor in July 1970. He and other longstanding advocates of the port could finally see the results of their work and look forward to the port's positive economic impact. Participants remember that thousands were on hand, amid a fair-like atmosphere of music, refreshments, and rides to tour the facilities by boat or, for the lucky ones, aboard the Goodyear blimp, and marvel at the transformation of ordinary lake frontage into an ultra-modern port. Speeches were given by various state and national leaders. Brochures prepared for the occasion described how the port—the culmination of a century-long dream—fit into national and world commercial patterns and the stimulus it would provide to the state's economy. Included in the press kit was a publication explaining the history of the port, particularly the intense struggle from the 1930s through the 1960s to get engineering and legislative support for the project.[1]

For all of its ballyhoo, the dedication in July 1970 was premature by perhaps as much as two years. Although limited shipping in and out had already begun, the port was not complete or really functional until late in 1972. Only one shipping berth—a total of thirty-one were called for in the master plan—was ready in 1970, and very few

The MV *Frank Purnell* unloading a cargo of aggregates, the first revenue-producing inbound cargo at Burns Waterway Harbor on May 1, 1970.

ground structures existed. The Port Commission staff occupied a warehouse headquarters building while waiting for construction of an office building. No permanent tenants had yet taken up their sites.[2]

By 1977, a dozen tenants had come to the port property, the eighth berth for serving its growing traffic was completed, a work boat harbor (for tugs and an Indiana State Police launch) was built, and both Manchester Line and Farrell Line vessels began, on an experimental basis, calling regularly at Burns Harbor.[3]

Among the port tenants were two stevedoring companies that utilized the huge transit shed (warehouse) erected by the Port Commission in 1972, as well as open storage areas. These companies hired their own laborers to handle both the general and specialized cargo moving through the port. Only a dozen stevedores worked full-time in 1972, but that number rose to almost forty in 1975 and to eighty in 1977, when total stevedore wages exceeded $1,700,000. There were also a number of specialized facilities for individual companies. A refrigerated warehouse, completed in 1978 and capable of maintaining temperatures from zero to twenty degrees below zero Fahrenheit, was available for the storage of perishable items, such as frozen meats or orange juice. A specially built salt-storage pad, intended for the temporary storage of ice-control salt shipped in from Canada, was also available for use in 1979. Built to current Environmental Protection Agency standards, the pad required special surface and sub-surface preparations, a wall to contain the salt within the proper area, and covers over the salt to control wind-blown losses. After delivery by self-unloader vessels, the salt could be taken by truck to Indiana highway and street departments for use on icy road surfaces.[4]

One of the more unusual operations that came to the port in its first decade was the Paul Dee Company's oyster shell processing plant. Shells from the Gulf of Mexico came by barge through the inland waterway system to Lake Michigan and on to Burns Harbor, where the Dee Company crushed and packaged them for use as calcium-rich chicken feed supplements used in great quantities on Indiana and other midwestern poultry farms.[5]

For traffic if not revenue impact, the most important commercial development in the 1970s was the decision in 1979 by Cargill, Inc., to locate a new grain elevator on port property. The commission promptly secured the necessary financing, and let construction contracts according to the required bidding procedures. Cargill's installation was in operation by 1981. The $21,500,000 facility had a 3,400,000 bushel storage capacity and was capable of annually moving 40,000,000 bushels of grain through the elevators and into ships headed for foreign markets.[6]

At the end of 1979, counting Cargill, which was not yet operational, Burns Harbor's dozen tenants all were contributing to the port's prosperity. The port also boasted of a seamen's center, housed at first in a mobile home and then in a more permanent building, that provided important services to visiting seamen, especially foreign nationals unfamiliar with the language and customs of the United States. The port's advanced sewage disposal system was the most comprehensive one along the Great Lakes in 1973. The system was equipped to handle not only a ship's on-board sewage but also its bilge water. In 1972, the commission received a commendation from the federal Environmental Protection Agency for the commitment to clean water that this special facility represented.[7]

By 1975, the port had begun to show an excess of income over expenditures (except for new construction), and by 1980 income exceeded expenditures by several hundred thousand dollars. In 1980, shipments into and from the port exceeded 1,205,000 tons of cargo; seventy-four percent resulted from ship traffic and twenty-six percent resulted from barge traffic.[8]

The port's income and traffic statistics, however, did not include harbor fee charges on the large number of barges and ore boats—the behemoths of the Great Lakes—which used the private docking facilities of the Bethlehem Steel Company. Revenue from this source had been expected and counted on in arguing for the port's construction

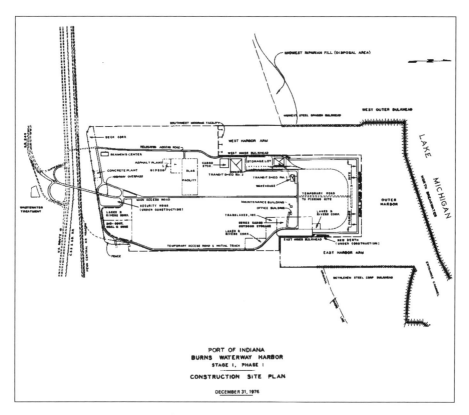

The construction site plan for Burns Waterway Harbor, 1976.

and making the case for its economic feasibility. The steel company maintained that such charges, at a harbor partially constructed and maintained by the federal government, violated the Northwest Ordinance, the U.S. Constitution, and various federal statutes, specifically the Rivers and Harbors Appropriation Act of 1884 that made navigation fees on publicly supported waterways illegal. Following repeated refusals by Bethlehem to pay the bills presented, the Indiana Port Commission filed suit in state court against the steel company in July 1971.[9]

The case was transferred in late 1971 to the U.S. District Court for the Northern District of Indiana, Hammond Division. It was delayed for years pending decisions by the Federal Maritime Commission regarding challenges initiated by Bethlehem Steel to the harbor service charge. When the Federal Maritime Commission held hearings on the matter in 1976, Clinton Green was retained by the commission to present its views, including the history of the dispute. After an unfavorable decision by an administrative judge in December 1986, the

Port Commission appealed to the United States Court of Appeals, Seventh Circuit, in Washington, D.C., but lost based on the finding that the harbor service fee violated the Rivers and Harbors Appropriation Act of 1884.[10]

This prolonged litigation proved to be enormously expensive—Commissioner Robert M. Schram remembers "wincing" when called upon to approve payments of the growing legal fees—but it was something about which the Port Commission, particularly its original members, felt very strongly. George Nelson, for example, while lobbying for the port, had always pledged to Indiana citizens and legislators that the steel companies would pay their fair share for the port, and that the port, moreover, would return to the state its entire investment in the port once an income was generated. Nelson considered the harbor fees legitimate, reasonable, and part of the steel company's fair share; he did not hesitate in pressing forward with the lawsuit.[11]

Like others, however, Nelson recognized that ore boats paying a harbor fee at Burns would lead to other lake shippers having to begin paying similar fees elsewhere, and he was troubled by the precedent-setting nature of the case. This case finally ended in 1988 when the Port Commission accepted the Court of Appeals ruling in late December 1987 invalidating the harbor service charges. The decision was a bitter pill for the commission after nearly two decades of contention. It was, however, a victory for the hallowed concept of free and open navigable waters as specified in both the Northwest Ordinance and the U.S. Constitution.[12]

The adverse decision also meant that Port Commission income would be more heavily based on other revenue sources, such as dockage and wharfage fees. Dockage fees commence at the time a vessel ties up at a dock and continue until it casts off; they depend upon a vessel's size and weight, either a flat rate (for smaller boats) or scaled according to a ship's net registered tonnage. Wharfage fees are based upon the cargo moving through the port and vary according to the value and type of commodity being handled. In addition, storage and special handling or special service fees might be levied. Another major source of income derives from lease or rental agreements. The rates are based upon the value of the land being occupied and, if applicable, the sums necessary to retire revenue bonds issued to erect the facilities being used by the tenant. Such rates, of course, must also reflect the commission's overhead expenses in providing utilities, roads, railroads, and administrative and security personnel. The labor and some of the equipment involved in handling the cargo or the containers is provided by stevedores, who collect their own fees.[13]

The Sverdrup & Parcel and Associates, Inc. *Interim Report* in 1964 suggested that surplus office space might be rented, but income from that and other sources has been limited at the agriculturally sterile port site at Burns Harbor. There is still a surplus of sand that must be disposed of to render the port site fully suitable for industry. From time to time, bids have been invited and some of this sand sold. Interest and dividends on investments have also been significant. Especially in the early years, they meant the difference between net gains or losses.[14]

There was also the matter of reimbursement from the federal government of the money provided by the state to build the outer harbor and entrance channel. The first federal reimbursements came in April and June 1970, when $11,950,713 was received. An additional $1,086,714 came during 1972, and two payments totaling $318,332 came during 1974 and 1975. After some haggling over the precise division of responsibility, it was finally determined in August 1975 that the federal share of port construction cost was $13,364,266. The remaining balance due was $8,507. Most of the initial large sum received went back into the state's general fund, as the original appropriation act of 1965 had specified. The $1,086,714 received in 1972 and the subsequent smaller payments, according to an amendment to the act in 1971, were diverted directly into the fund set up to build

Foreign ships at the new transit shed at Burns Waterway Harbor in 1972. River barges lie in the foreground; the remainders of sand dunes are visible to the right.

the Ohio River port (Southwind Maritime Centre) at Mount Vernon.[15]

Questions regarding income relate ultimately to traffic. During the early years of operations at Burns Harbor, there was a series of problems that, together, conspired to make progress slower than anticipated. First was the premature opening in 1970, rather than late 1972 when the first phase of construction was actually completed and Transit Shed No. 1 was available for use. There were other matters related to a general economic slowdown, deficiencies in both the St. Lawrence Seaway and local rail service, and various rate and port discriminations. Great Lakes traffic as a whole declined in the early 1970s. The new and modern facilities at Burns permitted its traffic, however, to grow slightly, but much less rapidly than if lake traffic generally had been bustling. Moreover, as time went on, the limitations of the St. Lawrence Seaway became more and more apparent. The seaway was constructed with lock chambers measuring 766 feet long by 80 feet wide, with a channel controlling depth of twenty-seven feet. After 1969, however, Great Lakes freighters 1,000 feet long were possible because of the construction of the Poe Lock at Sault Ste. Marie, which connected Lakes Huron and Superior. The smaller dimensions of the seaway reportedly resulted from the opposition of Atlantic and Gulf port interests, which feared the competition of a full-sized system and which had the power, if necessary, to block approval of the entire joint U.S.-Canadian project. It is also likely that the smaller lock sizes resulted from budget constraints. Moreover, the seasonal operation of the seaway made it difficult for Great Lakes ports to woo shippers away from existing routes overland to coastal ports that were available year-round.[16]

More serious, perhaps, but a problem more amenable to solutions locally, was the matter of rate discrimination based on the port's location just beyond the eastern limits of the Chicago Commercial Zone. Inclusion of the port within the zone would mean lower trucking rates, as well as the ability to negotiate rates, but it took six years to secure the change. The Interstate Commerce Commission's order extending the Chicago Commercial Zone to include Burns Harbor and the Bethlehem Steel Company became effective December 31, 1976. There was a similar situation regarding rail rates and the structure of the Chicago Shipping Zone. The problem was made more complicated by the fact that the New York Central Railroad, with tracks immediately adjacent to the port's overland entrance, was reluctant to share its port business with other roads. A second railroad with access to the port was needed so that competitive rates could develop.[17]

Burns Waterway Harbor under construction in 1977; aerial view looking southwest.

During the 1970s, the Port Commission spent much time trying to get Burns Harbor included on the U.S. Department of Agriculture's list of approved ports for the shipment of relief cargo under federal programs, such as Food for Peace, CARE, and AID. The traffic so generated was not enormous, but it was significant; moreover, it was labor-intensive cargo that would offer employment to the dockworkers. In 1973, after much effort on the part of Port Commission staff, the first relief shipment was made. A similar problem existed in 1972 when the U.S. government issued a list of approved ports-of-call on short-term notice for USSR vessels, but omitted Burns Harbor from the list. The Port Commission protested to appropriate federal agencies, such as the departments of state and agriculture. The oversight was subsequently corrected. According to Commissioner Schram, an appeal to the president via the state's congressional delegation corrected the oversight.[18]

All of the above efforts tied in with the special promotion efforts of the Port Commission to publicize the port to its own citizens and legislators, and to make shippers here and abroad aware of its expanding facilities. Individual port commissioners and staff members made frequent slide-illustrated presentations before business, civic, and professional groups. A considerable advertising campaign in the

**tide-ings**

**INDIANA PORT COMMISSION**
A LOOK AT WHAT'S HAPPENING AT
INDIANA'S PRESENT AND FUTURE PORTS

burns waterway harbor
portage, indiana

clark maritime centre
jeffersonville, indiana

southwind maritime centre
mount vernon, indiana

VOL. 3—NUMBER 20 • P.O. BOX 189 • PORTAGE, IND. 46368 • (219) 787-8636 • CABLE: INDYPORT • NOVEMBER 1974

## Port of Indiana Enjoys Shipping Boom In 1974

Despite the economic slump being experienced by other Great Lakes ports, business has been booming at the Port of Indiana-Burns Waterway Harbor where business has doubled so far this year as compared to the same period in 1973.

As of the end of October, 40 ships and 55 barges with a total cargo of 262,213 tons have used the Port of Indiana thus far in 1974.

At this point in 1973, 16 ships and 7 barges with a total cargo of 101,248 tons had loaded and unloaded at the port.

The situation at the Port of Indiana contrasts sharply with recent reports that other Great Lakes shipping facilities are suffering substantial business losses.

## Port Aids New Source of Energy

The Indiana Port Commission has licensed Carbon Energies, Inc., Hillside, Illinois, and Brown, Inc., of Michigan City, Indiana, to handle and transport coal screenings from Burns Waterway Harbor which are being received in barge loads originating from the area in and around St. Louis, Missouri. The coal screenings will be hauled to the Bailly Generating Station of Northern Indiana Public Service Company who have tested this type and source of Southern Illinois coal and found it will satisfactorily augment their present supply of coal.

Shipments of coal screenings are scheduled to initially total 180,000 tons and increase to approximately 300,000 tons annually at which time it is anticipated other plants of the utility will also use this fuel.

*The FORTUNA, Manchester Lines' container vessel*

## New Container Service Instituted At Port

A new, regularly scheduled container service has been instituted at Burns Waterway Harbor. The new service reaches areas in Great Britain.

In making the announcement to shippers, Manchester Lines stated that "In view of our very successful experience in utilizing the Burns Waterway Harbor during and since the serious labor difficulties, Manchester Lines has decided to continue servicing the Chicago Customs District and hinterland, utilizing the facilities of Tri-State Terminals Incorporated, located at the Port of Indiana-Burns Waterway Harbor.

It is felt that the quick dispatch and continuity of service gained by calling at a terminal located on Lake Michigan will improve overall transit time. It has also been found that the newer and less congested operation at Tri-State Terminals enables us to turn trucks around much more quickly to the considerable advantage of all concerned."

## Transit Shed No. 2 Nearly Completed

Construction of Transit Shed No. 2, the new 90,000 square foot facility at Burns Waterway Harbor is expected to be completed by the middle of November.

Although as yet unfinished, the current surge of business at the port has made it necessary to put the new building to use. Already the facility is more than two-thirds full of transit cargo which has recently arrived on foreign ships.

Furthermore, 100,000 square feet of outside storage has been recently paved in order to accommodate the business increase.

national press was mounted, new brochures were printed, and, often in cooperation with the Indiana Department of Commerce, increasing personal contacts with potential foreign customers were made. Governor Otis R. Bowen (1973-1981), successor to Governor Edgar D. Whitcomb (1969-1973), did not personally promote the ports as much as his predecessors had, leaving that major responsibility to Lieutenant Governor Robert D. Orr (1973-1981). Not only did Orr support an Ohio River port for southwestern Indiana, his own locality, but he also, as director of the state Department of Commerce, encouraged cooperation between that department and the Port Commission. He promoted the port personally on his many trips abroad.[19]

There were reasons for optimism in 1980 when Burns Harbor celebrated its tenth anniversary as an operating Great Lakes port. Its facilities were extensive, the traffic generated was growing, and various plans for expansion were underway. The port had begun to look like a true port. The commission also had resisted a plan to incorporate its operation within a state agency, the Indiana Department of Transportation. The Port Commission is operated as a business and is virtually free from political considerations, except for the mandated near-equal division between the political affiliations of those appointed as commissioners. The commission, therefore, is able to base its decisions upon business considerations and to keep the Indiana ports operating with a minimum of political involvement.[20]

Much credit for the successful debut of the Indiana Port Commission at Burns Harbor belongs to Jack P. Fitzgerald, who directed port affairs throughout the decade of the 1970s. He was ably assisted by Lewis B. Grafft, who had become the first full-time member of the Port Commission staff in 1964. Grafft served as deputy port director prior to his retirement in 1976. Another able Fitzgerald assistant was Ralph B. Joseph, an engineer, who oversaw the port construction process and then became the first director of operations. In 1980, when Fitzgerald retired to California, Joseph became the acting port director.[21]

There was also stability among the port commissioners. Albert L. Yeager, a businessman, perhaps frustrated by the political wrangling initially, was the only commissioner to retire from the board prior to the start of construction. Only one other man—Chairman James R. Fleming in 1969—retired during the 1960s. Yeager's replacement, Henry R. Sackett, was the next man to retire, after six years of service. The remainder of the initial appointees served into the mid-1970s or beyond. Given the retirements of the 1970s and a legislated increase in the number of commissioners from five to seven in 1975, six new commissioners came on board in the 1970s. Two of them remained in 1990, and all of the others but one (who served nine years) served at least ten years.[22]

As noted previously, the chairmanship in 1969 devolved upon Joseph N. Thomas, a vigorous Gary attorney, newly appointed to the board in that year. His tenure as chairman (1969-1974) was marked by gradual Burns Harbor development and the initiation of two Ohio River ports. His successor as chairman was William S. Young, a businessman from Plymouth and an enthusiastic weekend sailor, who carried on all three port efforts well. Two others deserve mention here in terms of significant contributions to the Port Commission during its initial decade of operation. Clinton Green, active in politics in the early 1960s, had returned as a consultant to the commission, while also working for Klein & Kuhn, the real estate firm

William S. Young served as an Indiana Port Commission commissioner, 1974-1984, and chairman, 1974-1983.

retained by the commission to handle its land acquisitions and, later, tenant lease arrangements. David G. Abraham, an economist and transportation specialist, who served as a consultant to the Indiana Port Commission throughout the 1970s and 1980s, also deserves special recognition. His expertise was invaluable regarding freight rates, Interstate Commerce Commission rules and regulations, sources of funding for special port activities, negotiations regarding the establishment of shipping zones—including, ultimately, Foreign Trade Zone applications for Indiana's two river ports—and other technical matters. In fact, during some periods following Fitzgerald's departure, Abraham might be said to have served as the *de facto* port director of the Port Commission.[23]

Much has already been said of the contributions of George Nelson. Following open-heart surgery, he reluctantly departed from the commission in 1976. His fellow commissioners paid special tribute to him with a resolution adopted in July 1976.[24]

While the foundations for a prosperous business at Lake Michigan were being laid, the Port Commission was also busy in the 1970s establishing the Ohio River port at Mount Vernon in southwestern Indiana, and trying, amid ongoing frustrations and delays, to do the same at Jeffersonville in southeastern Indiana.

George A. Nelson (third from left) shares with friends his Distinguished Hoosier award, presented in 1972 by Governor Edgar D. Whitcomb.

Southwind Maritime Centre in 1979; aerial view looking southwest.

Credit: Indianapolis *Star*, June 17, 1979.

# CHAPTER 7

# Accessing the Ohio River: Southwind Maritime Centre

As early as 1940, after the Indiana Board of Public Harbors and Terminals (IBPHT) was organized to seek a Lake Michigan deepwater port, individuals from the southern Indiana communities of Madison and Evansville expressed interest in establishing a public port in their localities, but nothing resulted. Likewise, later, when the Indiana General Assembly acted to boost economic development in northern Indiana, politicians from southern Indiana sought similar opportunities for economic development in their region. In 1961, the year the Port Commission replaced the IBPHT in order to build a public port on Lake Michigan, southern Indiana Democrat S. Hugh Dillin was president *pro tempore* of the Indiana Senate. John Van Ness, former state senator from Valparaiso, was lobbying for the port bill on behalf of his employer, Midwest Steel. Following discussions with leaders in both houses and Van Ness, Dillin agreed to rally Democratic support for the port project in return for Republican and northern Indiana support for various Democratic and southern Indiana concerns. These concerns included a large Monroe County reservoir project, flood control on all rivers and streams in Indiana, and improved navigation along the entire length of the Ohio River in Indiana. Similarly, in 1963, Governor Matthew E. Welsh (1961-1965), also from southern Indiana, included in his original $35,435,800 economic development

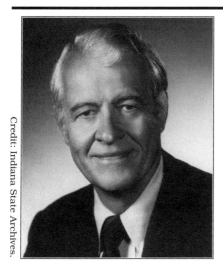

**"During my eight years as governor, and four years as United States Ambassador to Singapore, I came to realize the importance of public ports and maritime commerce to the economic health of states and nations.**

**"My predecessor in office, Otis Bowen, and I presided over the dedication of two public ports along the Ohio River, Clark Maritime Centre at Jeffersonville and Southwind Maritime Centre at Mount Vernon. Together, Indiana's three public ports have helped open Indiana to the global marketplace."**

*Robert D. Orr*
*Circa 1995*
*Governor of Indiana, 1981-1989*

fund plans for two bridges across the Ohio River and construction money for the port at Burns Harbor—a proposal explicitly balanced by regional interests. Moreover, the 1963 legislature amended the powers of the Port Commission to include constructing and operating an Ohio River port in Vanderburgh County. The bridges were funded in 1963; funding for the lake port came in 1965. By that time, it was evident that, at some point, the Port Commission would have to develop a lake and one or more river ports.[1]

Aside from geographical interests, such development would be needed because inland navigation improvements were underway within the country that were, in their total impact, even more significant and dramatic than completion of the St. Lawrence Seaway in 1959. The Ohio River, second only to the Mississippi River in the volume and importance of its traffic, was the focus of major improvements in the 1950s and 1960s. As mentioned previously, inland waterway transportation had declined precipitously in the late nineteenth century; railroads became the dominant form of transportation throughout the nation, but they were unable to handle the national traffic, a situation clearly not in the national interest. The report of President Theodore Roosevelt's (1901-1909) Inland Waterways Commission in 1908 recommended extensive improvements to the nation's rivers, and emphasized their importance to the national interest. Such improvements would serve multiple purposes—flood control and recreation as well as navigation and, therefore, competition for railroads. Congress responded with the Panama Canal Act of 1912, which among other things prohibited railroad control of water carrier operations through the Panama Canal or elsewhere, unless the Interstate Commerce Commission could determine that such control was in the public interest and would not lessen competition on the routes affected. Historians have considered this act to be the "legislative keystone" for the revival of inland water transportation. In section 500 of the Transportation Act of 1920, Congress declared that the policy of the United States was to "promote, encourage, and develop water transportation." Accordingly, in 1924, Congress created "the Inland Waterways Corporation for the purpose of carrying out the mandate and purpose of Congress as expressed in sections 201 ["Government-owned Boats on Inland Waterways"] and 500 of the Transportation Act" of 1920. The corporation, in fact, was to develop the transportation capabilities of the nation's rivers and other inland channels.[2]

By 1929, an Ohio River canalization project had been completed. This project involved the construction of new locks at each of forty-six dam sites designed to convert the river into a reliable nine-foot minimum depth channel for river craft. The locks, however, were only 110 by 600 feet in size and, by the 1950s, were clearly inadequate for the vast traffic on the Ohio River. Consequently, in 1955, an extensive modernization project was begun. Fewer but higher dams, accompanied by new and larger high-lift locks, were planned. Only nineteen locks and dams along the 981-mile course of the Ohio River would be needed, but the locks would be doubled in length, going from 600 to 1,200 feet long; the width remained at 110 feet. Actually, there would be two locks at each dam, the secondary ones having the dimensions in use previously—110 by 600 feet.[3]

The new lock dimensions accommodated the standard-size barge (35 by 195 feet) organized into tows three barges wide and five or six barges long. When the tows were six barges long, one barge in the last row would be removed to make room in the lock for both the tow and the towboat. Unlike tugboats, which ordinarily pull their loads, towboats push. Such tows, with barges designed and bound together so that they have the configuration and water resistance of a single vessel, result in an amazingly efficient and economic transportation system. In the 1970s, such tows averaged a cost of three to four mills per ton-mile, compared to railroad rates four to five times higher. Such tows could also be accommodated by the older 600-foot locks if necessary: the first three rows of barges could fill the lock first, and the final two or three rows and the towboat could go through on the second lift or descent.[4] This system, based largely on the enormous power and maneuverability of diesel-powered towboats and a series of new barge designs, marked a veritable revolution in the transportation potential of the nation's rivers and other inland waterways.[5]

Indiana businesses and industries on the Ohio River wanted to participate in the abundantly visible transportation boom taking place literally at their feet. By 1970, the Ohio River carried "millions upon millions of tons of freight to and from the [Ohio River] valley" and constituted "a tremendous asset of the Midwest and the nation."[6]

Beyond amendment of the Port Commission law in the 1963 regular session, little else happened regarding an Ohio River port until the end of the 1960s. The state's primary effort went toward Burns Harbor development, probably in part because a number of private Ohio River ports in Indiana, as well as one small public port at the Mead Johnson River-Rail-Truck Terminal and Warehouse in Evansville, already existed. No state action regarding additional public ports occurred until new legislators from Vanderburgh and Posey counties (H. Joel Deckard in the House and Robert D. Orr in the Senate) managed, in 1969, to get the powers of the Port Commission broadened again, thereby permitting the commission to establish a port in any county in the state bordering on the Ohio River. Moreover, Senator Orr found a way to get funding for a feasibility study for a southwest Indiana port. Recognizing that a separate bill for this purpose would have little chance of success, Orr convinced the director of the Department of Natural Resources to include $50,000 to be used for a port study in his budget proposal. The budget was approved, and soon the St. Louis engineering and consulting firm of Sverdrup & Parcel and Associates, Inc. had a new contract with the state of Indiana.[7]

Since Senator Orr represented both Vanderburgh and Posey counties, the study authorized an investigation to determine the most suitable site for a public port in the two counties. The majority of those

**"In 1969 and 1970, Sverdrup & Parcel did a study of where to locate a river port, in Posey or Vanderburgh County. I was on the Chamber in Mount Vernon and was appointed to a regional subcommittee to work with the engineering firm. There were four of us, and we pledged that wherever the site would be, we'd all support it. In September 1970, the Governor announced that the port would be located at Mount Vernon. Joe Thomas was chair of the Commission at that time, and he said I want somebody from Southwest Indiana on the Commission. I went up to Indianapolis and was sworn in by Governor Ed Whitcomb in November 1970."**

*William H. Keck*
*October 1997*
*Indiana Port Commission*
*commissioner, 1970-1991,*
*and chairman, 1984*

involved probably expected the site to be in Vanderburgh County, if not Evansville itself. The Sverdrup & Parcel engineers concluded in their feasibility report, however, that the best high-level land needed for industrial park development adjacent to the port could be found most cheaply in Posey County. The river configuration at potential spots in both counties was another important factor in the site recommendation. An unsuitable main channel location and strong currents at the Evansville site contrasted with an island-protected site suitable in all regards at Mount Vernon. The island, Mount Vernon Towhead, moreover, provided a convenient barge-fleeting spot that is still heavily used in the 1990s.[8]

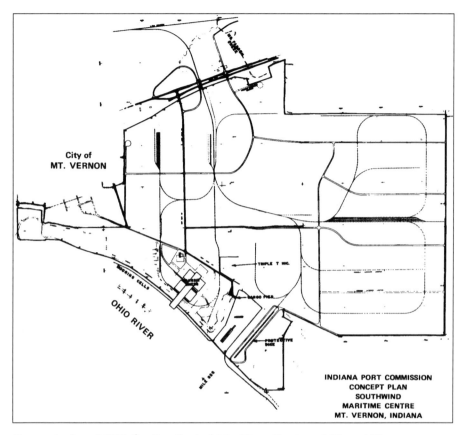

Concept plan, 1976, for Southwind Maritime Centre at Mount Vernon.

The Sverdrup & Parcel engineers gave close consideration to three sites, two in Posey County on either side of Mount Vernon and one in Vanderburgh County slightly downriver from Evansville. Site two, adjacent to Mount Vernon's eastern corporate limits, was the one recommended. Preliminary plans were prepared for a modern river port, equipped with grain, coal, and general-purpose dry and liquid bulk transfer facilities as well as an inner harbor and marina. In a report released on September 1, 1970, engineers estimated a total cost of $13,200,000 for the first phase of land acquisition, site preparation, and construction of the basic port facilities.[9]

Now attention shifted back from engineering to politics, sometimes referred to as the art of persuasion. Fortunately for port promoters in southwestern Indiana, the newest member of the Port Commission proved to be a master of that art. William H. Keck, appointed to the commission in the summer of 1970 by Governor Edgar D. Whitcomb (1969-1973), was an automobile dealer in Mount Vernon.[10] Together with Senator Orr and Mount Vernon businessman Arthur W. Bayer, who already operated a barge fleeting and repair service, along with a good many others from the "pocket" area of southern Indiana, Keck arranged to make the locale, the port plans, and the opportunities it represented to the area and to the state as widely known as possible. One strategy used was a series of "fly-ins" that brought influential decision-makers from all over the state to Mount Vernon. These fly-ins occasionally used a sodded airstrip, later removed, located on the potential port site, and featured river cruises and lunches aboard a ferry barge. Such activities supported efforts elsewhere to let Indiana take better advantage of the Ohio River. New developments in inland shipping made direct shipments from foreign ports feasible. These developments included advances in containerization, such as LASH (lighter aboard ship) and SeaBee (sea barge carrier) vessels, which allowed transshipments between ocean-going vessels and river barges without unloading the cargo. The Southwind Maritime Centre, as the Mount Vernon port came to be known, was a potential "world export-import center."[11]

At the groundbreaking ceremony for Southwind Maritime Centre in 1973 are (from left) Indiana Port Commission Chairman Joseph N. Thomas, Governor Otis R. Bowen, Lieutenant Governor Robert D. Orr, and Port Commission Commissioner William H. Keck.

The Indiana General Assembly in 1971, which convened just months following release of the Sverdrup & Parcel report, promptly funded the river port project, voting an initial $1,000,000 for land acquisition and other preliminaries. The legislature also directed that the remaining federal reimbursements for the Burns Harbor project—approximately $1,300,000 was still outstanding—would go to the river port. Port Director Jack P. Fitzgerald, although new to the job in Indiana and unfamiliar with the area, undertook the earliest negotiations for land. At Commissioner Keck's suggestion, he first approached Joseph Hodge, a native of Posey County and a respected farmer there. Hodge not only agreed to sell the needed land that he owned but also became an unofficial good-will ambassador for the entire project. Keck expressed pride that all of the land acquired for the port was obtained with only one resort to condemnation proceedings.[12]

During 1971 and 1972, steps were taken to begin construction as soon as funds became available. By 1973, the Indiana General Assembly had voted $3,700,000 in construction funds, and work was soon underway. The first contract for preliminary site preparation went to the Dyer Construction Company of Dyer, Indiana.[13]

Before construction could begin in 1973 a preliminary archaeological assessment was required of the proposed barge bay or inlet area at McFadden Creek. Two small prehistoric sites were discovered. Both were destroyed by subsequent construction and development.[14]

Ground was broken on June 1, 1973 for the Mount Vernon port. Governor Otis R. Bowen (1973-1981), accompanied by his lieutenant governor, Robert D. Orr, who had played a vital role in the project already, headed the list of dignitaries. Bowen called Southwind Maritime Centre a "significant milestone" in southwestern Indiana's economic development; it was also proof that the perceived traditional neglect by state government of this area was over. He predicted that the port would be an "unparalleled economic asset" to the state. Lieutenant Governor Orr also spoke, praising in particular the efforts of state Representative H. Joel Deckard, formerly of Mount Vernon, on behalf of the port. Port Commission Chairman Joseph N. Thomas and its member from Mount Vernon, William Keck, also praised Deckard. The four men then simultaneously removed the first shovelsful of earth, after which they attended a large luncheon-reception at the Western Hills Country Club.[15]

Covering the groundbreaking, the Mount Vernon *Democrat* observed that

Southwind Maritime Centre under construction in 1977; aerial view looking northwest.

> Supporters of the project are quick to point out that the very fact that Southwind embraces some 1,110 acres of ground adjacent to the Ohio River, more than 800 of which are high, flat and flood-free, makes it unique as an industrial location attraction.
>
> The Southwind site is the last major high bank, flood-free, undeveloped industrial site on the entire stretch of the Ohio River from Pittsburgh to Cairo.

The article also noted that "every major, heavy industry feels it must have all modes of transportation available to it, and water compelled freight rates in particular," made Southwind a desirable spot for industries wishing to expand along the Ohio River. The assertion of Port Commission Chairman Thomas was reiterated: "the commission will return every dollar to the state through industrial leasing revenues."[16]

Within a year the first cargo pier was completed, and within two more years the port began limited shipping activities. While the commission was building its infrastructure of roads and railroads, water and sewer lines, and other utilities, the state cooperated by completing a four-lane highway between Mount Vernon and Evansville. The highway made the port truly multi-modal, with good access by rail

The Behimer and Kissner grain facility at Southwind Maritime Centre in
1982; it was completed in 1978.

Barges being positioned to receive cargo from the Behimer and Kissner
grain elevator at Southwind Maritime Centre in 1984.

At Southwind Maritime Centre, the state-of-the-art coal transfer and marine facility completed by MAPCO, INC. in 1982 featured a half-mile long conveyor belt system; aerial view looking northeast. The conveyor system goes from the center of the photograph to the river at the far right.

(CSX system), road, and water. Ideally, the port also needed a second railroad serving its customers, and another four-lane highway running north and south, which would provide truckers easy access to and from Interstate 64, running through northern Posey County. There is also interest in a highway connection to Kentucky, via a new bridge over the Ohio River in the Evansville-Mount Vernon area. The Port Commission was unable to get support for this idea from the Indiana Toll Bridge Commission in the 1980s; the commission's updated 1973 feasibility study still showed insufficient traffic potential. Such a bridge was considered a possibility later, as part of an interstate connection between Indianapolis and Memphis by way of Posey County.[17]

By 1976, Southwind had its first tenant—Triple T Fertilizer Company of Vincennes, Indiana, a large shipper of dry and liquid fertilizer. Three more firms leased property in 1977. By 1980, the six tenants at Southwind included Behimer and Kissner, Inc., whose grain elevator (the capacity of which reached 2,600,000 bushels by 1982) dominated the port landscape, and Timber Export Products, Inc., engaged in shipping logs from its docks in the inner harbor. Stevedoring services for general cargo, as well as barge fleeting and related

The Southwind Maritime Centre was dedicated in June 1979. At the operator's booth of the crane are (from left) Gene Marksberry of the International Union of Operating Engineers, Local 181, Robert Thiem of Mount Vernon Barge Service, Inc., and Governor Otis R. Bowen. Standing below (from left) are Indiana Port Commission commissioners Norman E. Pfau, Jr., Quentin A. Blachly, Harry F. Zaklan, William H. Keck, William E. Babincsak, William S. Young, and Robert M. Schram.

services, were provided by Mount Vernon Barge Service, Inc., operated by port promoter Arthur W. Bayer. Significantly, MAPCO, INC., an energy company with headquarters in Tulsa, Oklahoma, announced plans in 1980 to build a coal transfer and marine facility at Southwind. MAPCO's state-of-the-art operation, featuring a loop railroad from which bottom-vented cars could be emptied without stopping, and a half-mile long conveyor belt from which barges could be loaded, was expected to ship some 2,500,000 tons of coal a year. This facility was completed in 1982 and since then has been a prime factor in the remarkable tonnages shipped through Southwind. Most of this coal, from MAPCO's own mines in Illinois and Kentucky, was destined (via the Ohio and Mississippi rivers, the Gulf Intracoastal Waterway, and then train) for the Seminole Power Plant in Palatka, Florida, with which MAPCO had negotiated a twenty-seven year contract.[18]

Although traffic began in 1976, and construction was completed in 1978, official dedication ceremonies did not take place until 1979. By then, Southwind was in full swing and well on its way to becoming the star of the port system in terms of through-put tonnage. Mark

The *William Jeffrey Bayer*, a switch boat, was added to the Mount Vernon Barge Service, Inc., fleet in 1990.

Allen, hired initially in 1974 by the commission as an international trade representative to solicit cargo, had been transferred in 1977 to manage Southwind. An extremely knowledgeable and affable waterways man, he proved to be equally effective in promoting the new port and attracting new business to its docks. His sudden death in 1984, remarked upon in the minutes of the commission, represented a "severe blow" for the Port Commission and left "a great void."[19]

Others built upon the foundations Allen had helped to lay. In August 1984, Chris V. Kinnett of Jeffersonville was employed to serve as port manager of Southwind and of Clark Maritime Centre, then under construction at Jeffersonville. An experienced transportation specialist, Kinnett devoted his time primarily to marketing activities for both ports.[20] The 1983 tonnage figures of 1,877,122 tons at Southwind nearly doubled the next year, reaching a total of 3,538,419 tons. The traffic consisted, as noted previously, primarily of coal, grain, logs, and dry and liquid fertilizers. The Cargill company was now the major shipper of fertilizers, having assumed the lease and facilities of Triple T Fertilizer Company in 1984. In addition, Behimer and Kissner was then operating a pellet mill at the site, salvaging grain dust for combination with milled grain products to create pelletized animal feed. This growth in traffic had required new harbor dolphins. At the same time the Port Commission made other improvements to the port's infrastructure, which has allowed, for example, regular container shipments of appliance parts from Brazil for Whirlpool Corporation in Evansville, via New Orleans and the inland waters. Following years of study and effort by the Port Commission staff, Foreign Trade Zone status for the port was achieved in 1991.[21]

The chief problem at Southwind involves an apparent design flaw. The decision to let McFadden Creek empty into the inner harbor, the most practicable alternative at the time, has resulted in significant siltation of the harbor. It had been expected that the creek, particularly at times of high water, would flush sediment carried into the harbor back out into the river, but this has not happened. Many cubic yards of material flowed into the harbor during the first five and a half years, when the problem was first studied, and a permanent solution, such as relocation of the creek, is still being sought. In the meantime, infrequent dredging of the area is required. In all other ways, the layout has worked well, and the performance of the port has far exceeded expectations.[22]

Clark Maritime Centre under construction in 1984; aerial view looking southwest.

# CHAPTER 8

## A Second Ohio River Port: Clark Maritime Centre

If things went well at Southwind, the opposite was true at Indiana's southeastern port, named Clark Maritime Centre as the result of a contest by local chambers of commerce in 1973. Much like the Southwind project, at the beginning everything seemed to fall into place. The Indiana General Assembly appropriated funds for a feasibility study in 1971—$50,000 was made available, as had been the case with Southwind earlier, and the firm of Sverdrup & Parcel and Associates, Inc. got its third major port study contract from Indiana the same year. The company carefully followed its mandate to investigate Indiana's Ohio River shoreline from the Ohio state line to the mouth of Pigeon Creek in Warrick County, near Evansville. Five sites—at Aurora, Madison, Jeffersonville, New Albany, and Tell City—were identified for further study, according to a set of pre-determined criteria involving existing industrialization, work force, rail and highway access, potential for waterborne commerce growth, and community support. Only two of the five sites—Jeffersonville and New Albany—met the minimum standards. Both were in the "Louisville Economic Area," as defined by the U.S. Department of Commerce, and both were analyzed in great detail.[1]

"A port serves but one purpose," the study noted, "the transfer of freight from one mode of transport to another," and that transfer, to be economical, must be "fast and efficient." More specifically, the site preferred should be convenient to users, have adequate land (200 to 300 acres for cargo handling, and up to 1,000 acres more for water-related industrial development), be located above the high water mark of record (in this case, the 1937 flood), be near, but away from, the main river channel, have or have the potential for excellent rail and road connections, and have essential utility services available at reasonable costs. Based on all of the above factors, Jeffersonville was chosen over New Albany; the site was to be northeast of the city in the vicinity of Sixmile Island, which would provide a natural protection for the port and offer barge fleeting possibilities, just as Mount Vernon Towhead does at Southwind. The chief limitation of the site was inadequate highways, but existing plans for extending Interstate 265, perhaps even across the river into Kentucky, would alleviate that problem.[2]

Sverdrup & Parcel's *Southeast Indiana Ohio River Port Feasibility Report* was released to the public on June 29, 1972; it estimated the first-phase development costs at $14,900,000, slightly higher than Southwind because of higher land values and the need to bring some points on the site above flood stage level. Moreover, based upon a study of port prospects and a regional economic analysis, the proposals for initial site development encompassed facilities for general cargo (including steel and steel products), bulk commodities, and a separate grain terminal. Extensive benefits would flow from the port's construction, to the farm community in terms of higher net income and to the state in general in terms of new jobs and increased tax revenues. There existed, the economic analysts believed, "considerable demand for water-oriented industrial sites . . . and, over a period of five to ten years, the lands can be leased and developed for the benefit of industry and for repayment of the port's initial cost to the state."[3]

The report also listed the requirements in order to get started—surveys and maps, land appraisals and title searches, subsurface investigations, soil tests, and river soundings—and the local, state, and federal agencies that had to issue permits before construction could begin.[4] The permit process seemed routine, if laborious, and a start was made. The 1973 Indiana General Assembly granted $1,750,000 for initial land purchases and related expenses, and that process began. Soon, however, in a situation that must have reminded Port Commission veterans of the Burns Harbor struggle, a vocal opposition emerged. As with the Burns Harbor site, several of the objectors were out-of-state people—in this case Kentuckians—who expressed environmental concerns, but whose arguments supported

**"With the construction of this new river port, in conjunction with the Southwind Maritime Centre some 231 miles downriver in Posey County near Mt. Vernon, a vital new waterborne transportation link is added to our network."**

*Otis R. Bowen*
*July 1973*
*Governor of Indiana, 1973-1981*

the economic interests of the Ohio River port at Louisville.

The initial reception, on both sides of the river, to the Jeffersonville port proposals had been either enthusiastic or indifferent, but there was little opposition. When port director Jack P. Fitzgerald toured the port site in December 1972 and spoke with area reporters, his remarks received banner headlines in the Louisville *Times.* Fitzgerald emphasized the economic impact of the development on the entire greater Louisville area. The Ohio River, for all its antiquity and already heavy use, was still "in its infancy compared to other rivers of the world," according to Fitzgerald, and enormous growth in river traffic was coming. Not only new locks and dams, but also "revolutionized" new carrying vessels were keys to this growth. Fitzgerald cautioned, however, in words that proved to be truer than he could have anticipated, "that port construction is a slow, painstaking process." Nevertheless, some months later, after the legislature had appropriated initial construction funds, Governor Otis R. Bowen (1973-1981) was in Jeffersonville and praised the port, reportedly calling it "a giant step toward economic development of one of the state's finest natural resources: the Ohio River."[5]

Obviously, neither Fitzgerald nor Bowen expected problems with the formal environmental assessments already underway. The Corps of Engineers, however, was increasingly sensitive to the types of environmental concerns that had led to the National Environmental Policy Act of 1969, which created the Environmental Protection Agency; the Corps had established its own high-level Environmental Advisory

Viewing the proposed site for a state-owned port along the Ohio River southeast of Jeffersonville are (from left) Indiana Port Commission Chairman Joseph N. Thomas; Indiana state Representatives Maurice H. McDaniel (R-Floyd County) and Richard B. Wathen (R-Clark County); and Governor Otis R. Bowen, who designated the site by proclamation on June 25, 1973.

Committee. The Corps' Louisville district office soon determined that its preliminary environmental assessment had to be elevated to a full-scale Environmental Impact Statement. This study would be prepared by the Corps according to procedures that included a public hearing and "sign-offs" by state and federal agencies. The process also required that a preliminary draft Environmental Impact Statement be submitted by the Port Commission. The Corps estimated that the entire process would add from nine to thirty months to the time required for issuing a construction permit. All of the details regarding the Environmental Impact Statement were worked out and agreed to in September 1974, following meetings with the Louisville district engineer and members of Governor Bowen's staff. As announced by Bowen on September 10, the Port Commission unanimously supported the procedure, believing it to be "in the public interest." Bowen also confirmed Port Commission plans to seek alternative sources for fill material, thereby eliminating the need to dredge in the vicinity of Sixmile Island.[6]

The elaborate review process involved model studies by Purdue University scientists and Sverdrup & Parcel staff and an archaeological assessment. As at Southwind, the Glenn A. Black Laboratory of Archaeology at Indiana University, Bloomington, then headed by Professor James H. Kellar, was hired to conduct this assessment. Sverdrup & Parcel and the Louisville district office of the Corps of Engineers worked together on the development of the Environmental Impact Statement from 1974 through 1977, which incorporated Kellar's archaeological findings. After the last local hearings with representatives of the U.S. Fish and Wildlife Service, the Corps' district office forwarded its recommendations to the division office in Cincinnati. The division engineer reviewed the Environmental Impact Statement and forwarded the recommendations to the chief engineer in Washington in February 1977.[7]

While these studies were underway, outcries of opposition to the entire concept began, particularly among the people of Louisville, where hostility toward the port had begun to mount. Lieutenant Governor Robert D. Orr took the lead in trying to achieve what he called, in a note to Governor Bowen, a "Detente with Kentucky." At one point in October 1975, while in Kentucky on another matter, Orr called upon Cyrus MacKinnon, a friend at the Louisville *Courier-Journal* offices, a center of port criticism, in an attempt "to disabuse the opposition from what may be a misunderstanding" of our intentions at the port site. Orr believed, as did many others, that some of Kentucky's resistance to the Clark Maritime Centre stemmed from "the fact that Mrs. Barry [Mary] Bingham, Sr. lives in a sizable mansion on a hilltop right across the river from Indiana's port." She and other influential people in Kentucky were leading the battle, because of environmental as well as personal concerns. Orr stressed in a letter to MacKinnon that the project would produce "unbelievable economic benefits to Kentucky as well as Indiana," and suggested in a memorandum to Governor Bowen that "sensible communication on the subject, rather than hostile verbal bombardment" could resolve the problem.[8]

Orr's personal intervention at least may have led to a public discussion of the issues in the Louisville *Courier-Journal* five months later. Orr and state Representative Richard B. Wathen from Jeffersonville presented their case for the port; Mary Bingham and Lois Troyer, both identified as active in environmental circles, presented their arguments against it. Wathen first reviewed the legislative and financial history of the port proposal; he then described Kentucky Governor Wendell Ford's "grandstand play for his senatorial campaign," using Kentucky state funds to buy Sixmile Island from its Indiana owners for an amount in excess of $100,000, thereby keeping it from Hoosier developers. Influential citizens of Louisville, with homes facing the river, Wathen added, were also opposed to the new river port: such "objectors" have delayed the project for more than a year, while land costs have skyrocketed. Jobs are at stake, he concluded, for men and women in both states, because the river port will serve both states.[9]

Orr provided a statement from the perspective of state government, suggesting that "port facilities are as much a public enterprise as are roads and bridges" and that they lead to economic development and new jobs. He also explained the careful nature of the site selection process, and the economic and technical factors that made the Jeffersonville site "clearly preferable to the alternative site downriver from New Albany." Finally, he pointed to the increased residential developments in the area, "largely populated by Kentuckians," and said the taxes needed to pay for schooling and other necessary services required an expanded industrial base.[10]

Just as Wathen and Orr focused on economic arguments and ignored environmental issues, Troyer and Bingham focused on environmental arguments and ignored economic issues. From the environmentalists' perspective, the negative factors of water, air, and noise pollution, and the resultant erosion and navigation hazards in an already overcrowded, environmentally fragile area would be devastating. Troyer made effective use of the Draft Environmental Impact Statement, prepared by the U.S. Army Corps of Engineers (with data and analyses from Sverdrup & Parcel), quoting its findings, for example, regarding run-offs from the port site during construction. Bingham also revealed her familiarity with the draft document, but stressed instead adverse "quality of life" impacts if the port was built. She pointed out that now the state of Kentucky owned Sixmile Island, which has "great value as a recreational resource for Louisville and Jefferson County, and because of the archaeological importance of the forty-three prehistoric sites to be found there." Both women concluded that the alternative site at New Albany, below the Falls of the Ohio, would be a preferable site, with far fewer adverse effects on the environment and recreational uses.[11]

It is unlikely that either side changed its views following this and similar exchanges at various public hearings, but, in the meantime, project delays continued. In January 1976, Kellar reported his preliminary findings regarding the "prehistoric potential" of the port site.

The Indiana University team had discovered

> prehistoric material representing a nearly 4000 year time span
> from about 3000 B.C. to A.D. 1000. All of these occupations are
> covered by alluviation ranging in depth from 1 1/2 to 4 feet and,
> therefore, they have been undisturbed by 150 years of cultiva-
> tion. Because preservation in several of these sites is exception-
> ally good, they constitute documents of significant value. Mini-
> mally, their destruction without investigation would be a tragedy.

Consequently, Kellar recommended a salvage program at a cost of
$240,000. His cover letter to the report noted that "federal laws con-
cerning environmental assess-
ment come into play," specifically National Park Service guidelines regarding the evaluation of
sites "in terms of the criteria
established for the National Register of Historic Places Nomination. We have recommended and
the National Park Services [sic]
concurs that a portion of the
Clark Maritime project area be
so nominated."[12]

Kellar had rejected an earlier
request, received through Port
Commission engineer C. Thomas
Bagley, that the National Register nomination not go forward
for fear it would jeopardize the
entire project. Kellar's responsibility in the matter was clear. He

C. Thomas Bagley, Port Commission
engineer, circa 1975.

pointed out, however, that to date the President's Council on Historic
Preservation "has recommended salvage rather than preservation for
prehistoric occupations." Kellar also stated that he personally had no
objection to the port, which would have a positive effect on the state's
economy, but he did object to "watching bulldozers rip up in uncon-
trolled fashion significant portions of Indiana's past."[13]

The Port Commission minutes for January 1976 reported, with no
elaboration, that Kellar's "recommendations if implemented could
seriously compromise the Clark Maritime Centre" project. The Port
Commission voted to meet as soon as possible with Joseph Cloud,
director of the Indiana Department of Natural Resources, through
whom, as head of the state's historic preservation office, National Reg-

"**Throughout my twenty years of service to the state of Indiana, I was impressed with the non-partisanship of the Port Commission and our ability to operate as an on-going business without the political maneuvering and bureaucratic interference sometimes imposed by government. Members of our Commission were usually independent in thinking, and their first concern was for what was best for Indiana. Probably the biggest highlight of my two decades with the Commission was the opening of the Clark Maritime Centre after many years of litigation and opposition from the state of Kentucky.**"

*Norman E. Pfau, Jr.*
*October 1997*
*Indiana Port Commission*
*commissioner, 1975-1995*

ister nominations were transmitted to the National Park Service. A four-page "Memorandum for Record" describes the tense meeting that took place in Cloud's office on February 3, 1976. There were thirteen people attending—including representatives from the Port Commission, Governor Bowen's office, and the Jeffersonville Chamber of Commerce. Several legislators and new Port Commission member, Norman E. Pfau, Jr. from Jeffersonville, also attended. A businessman and manufacturer interested in his area's economic development, Pfau was a long-time advocate of a port there.[14]

Port Director Fitzgerald opened the meeting by suggesting "that any forces that are attempting to sacrifice the proposed port for an archaeological dig should be checked," and that compromise, providing something for each side, was needed. Port Commission Chairman

Attending the Clark Maritime Centre groundbreaking ceremonies in 1982 are (from left) Indiana Port Commission Commissioner Norman E. Pfau, Jr.; Governor Robert D. Orr; Port Commission Chairman William S. Young; U.S. Representative Lee H. Hamilton (D-Indiana); and U.S. Senator Richard G. Lugar (R-Indiana).

William S. Young said that "Dr. Kellar should have worked more closely with us," and expressed concern that preservation, not salvage, might be required. William J. Watt, from the governor's office, suggested that, since "the whole Ohio River reeks with archaeological sites," they should be "put in priority," and Representative Wathen offered the opinion that he "believed salvage to be a reasonable way to go." Cloud pointed out that the nomination of the "Clark Maritime Archaeological District" would be taken up by the "State historic preservation Screening Board" the next day, and that Kellar was a member of the board, having been recommended by the governor and appointed by the Secretary of the Interior.[15]

The Clark Maritime Archaeological District nomination was forwarded by the state to the National Park Service, on Kellar's recommendation. As Kellar had predicted, an extensive archaeological mitigation, or salvage operation, was required, the estimated cost of which reached $223,800. The Port Commission worked out an agreement by which the National Park Service would pay sixty-nine percent of these expenses and the Port Commission thirty-one percent.[16]

On May 8, 1976, the Corps of Engineers conducted a well-attended public hearing on the port proposal in the Jeffersonville High School. Many local interests turned out to hear the proceedings, which elicited surprisingly few new negative comments. The chief opposition spokesman was Jefferson County (Kentucky) Judge Todd Hollenbach; neither federal nor state of Kentucky agencies made oral presentations. The *Annual Report* of the Port Commission for 1977 contains no mention of the Clark Maritime Centre; there is no section comparable to "PROGRESS . . . at Burns Harbor" and "PROGRESS . . . at Southwind Maritime Centre." In a review the following year, after still more delay, Chairman Young stated that

> the Commission very much regrets that it was unable to begin construction of Clark Maritime Centre in 1978. While the Office of the Chief of the U.S. Army Corps of Engineers indicated during the year that it favors issuing the needed construction permit, other federal agencies and Kentucky special interests placed new hurdles in the Commission's path. All the while the cost of construction continues to escalate and the citizens of Southeastern Indiana are deprived of a facility that can contribute to their well-being.[17]

Finally, in June 1979, the Corps of Engineers issued the long-awaited construction permit. A few months earlier in February, however, the state of Kentucky had filed suit in federal court claiming ownership of the Ohio River up to the Indiana shoreline. If ruled valid, such a claim would effectively prevent port development at Clark and perhaps wreck the port already in operation at Southwind. Again the Clark project was put on hold while the case was litigated.[18]

The project would have been delayed for other reasons anyway. The Corps of Engineers' construction permit was conditional upon further archaeological mitigation, which was handled by Resource Analysts, Inc. of Bloomington, Indiana and completed in 1982. In addition, there was the suit, filed in 1979 against the Port Commission, which challenged its selection of the Jeffersonville site over one less ecologically damaging at New Albany. This suit forced the Port Commission to restudy the matter and submit a broader Environmental Impact Statement that considered alternative sites for the port. By 1982, both issues in litigation were settled in favor of the Port Commission. The U.S. Court of Appeals, Sixth Circuit, in 1981 validated the site selection, and the U.S. Supreme Court accepted a special master's report regarding the boundary issue. Although Kentucky's boundary at the time of its statehood in 1792 did include all of the Ohio River, the issue focused on where the river boundary was located in 1792. Surveys indicated that the river's mean low water mark in 1792 was several yards away from the Indiana shoreline in 1979, thereby giving Indiana control of its own waterfront and the Port Commission clearance to proceed with Clark.[19]

With evident relief, but with little comment, the Port Commission's 1982 *Annual Report* notes that the year's most significant development was the groundbreaking ceremony for Clark Maritime Centre. Construction was soon underway, starting a full dozen years after the initial legislative appropriation for the project. One of the earliest and largest major construction contracts awarded went to the Hall Contracting Corporation of Louisville, Kentucky. This award validated both the integrity of the bidding process and provided an example of mutual benefits through interstate cooperation. Once begun, things proceeded rapidly, and the Indiana General Assembly did its part to keep the work on schedule. Additional appropriations in 1983 and 1984 enabled the port to be ready for business in 1985. The port's first cargoes were shipped during the month of August.[20]

Three major tenants soon came to the port: Merchants Grain, Inc., a large shipper of agricultural commodities; Eagle Steel Company, a specialty steel firm; and Clark Stevedores and Riggers, Inc., a newly organized local firm established to handle general and bulk cargoes at

The ribbon cutting at the official opening of Interstate 265 in the summer of 1994, providing direct access to Clark Maritime Centre, featured (from left) New Albany Mayor Douglas B. England; Jeffersonville Mayor Raymond J. Parker; Indiana Port Commission Vice Chairman Norman E. Pfau, Jr.; Indiana state Senator Kathy Smith (D-Floyd County); Governor Evan Bayh; and Indiana state Representative James L. Bottorff (R-Clark County).

the port. A major distinction of the Clark Maritime Centre as of 1985 was its heavy-lift capabilities, with huge cranes powerful enough to lift up to 200 tons on docks capable of supporting 450 tons. Almost as soon as this machinery was installed, it was put to the test. Massive 90- to 100-ton automobile presses from West Germany, intended for use in the General Motors Truck and Bus Division plant in Indianapolis, arrived by barge in the fall of 1985. Successfully lifted onto a small fleet of ninety-six wheel trucks, the presses arrived at their destination without incident.[21]

In April 1988, formal dedication ceremonies marked the completion of the state's third public port. In 1989, Clark shipped over 653,000 tons of cargo, up thirty-three percent from the previous year. The prospects for continued traffic development were good. The port was well designed, had available land for industrial use, the basic infrastructure was in place, and it was more favored with complementary transportation systems than the other ports in the system: two competing railroads (CSX and Conrail), and an interstate highway extension (I-265), which terminates at the port's northern entrance and which is connected to I-65 northwest of the port. Indeed, Clark's potential—largely unrealized during its first half decade—was unusually bright. Commission Chairman Quentin A. Blachly wrote in 1985, prior to the Jeffersonville port's opening, that cargo through it would "quickly exceed that of each of the other ports."[22]

# CHAPTER 9

# Moving to the Future

The completion of Clark Maritime Centre on the Ohio River at Jeffersonville in 1985 essentially shifted the major focus of the Indiana Port Commission from construction to operations. After more than two decades of sometimes frenetic construction activity, the Port Commission in the late 1980s and early 1990s turned to consolidation. Construction efforts that had consumed the time of Port Commission and staff since the 1960s were now secondary.

After 1985, the Port Commission placed new emphasis on securing tenants for the three public ports, strategic planning, port promotion to both the Indiana and maritime communities, and public relations. The commission unveiled an improved, more visually attractive newsletter, *Indiana Portside,* and began producing videotapes useful in publicizing the state's public port system to a variety of audiences. Staff increased participation in domestic and international trade shows and missions, many sponsored under the auspices of the St. Lawrence Seaway Development Corporation in Washington, D.C. The Port Commission also hosted port open houses and Hoosier Hospitality Days celebrations as a way to increase the visibility of the three ports in the public eye.

Still, most Hoosiers considered themselves residents of an essentially landlocked state. Robert D. Kraft, Port Commission executive director, complained in 1987 that when he introduced himself as the "port commissioner of Indiana," people often thought that he was the state's "pork commissioner." The public was still unaware, Kraft added, "that Indiana is a major participant in world trade."[1]

Kraft's complaint aside, many in the state's business and government community from the governor on down were working to change the perception of Indiana as a landlocked state. Governor Robert D. Orr (1981-1989), whose support during his first term for Clark Maritime Centre had been critical in getting the Ohio River port off the ground, did much to increase awareness of the ports' potential, both at home and abroad. Orr was instrumental in encouraging the Port Commission to continue its joint marketing efforts with the Indiana Department of Commerce, which he had headed during two terms as lieutenant governor from 1973 to 1981.

Orr also insisted that the Indiana Port Commission relocate its headquarters from Burns Harbor to Indianapolis. The move made sense on two counts. Given the commission's statewide responsibility for three ports, an Indianapolis location was a signal to the maritime community that centralization of port operations was a reality. The move also increased the Port Commission's visibility statewide while increasing its access to the levers of power in the state capital.

Port Commission staff made the move from Burns Harbor to the second floor of the Harrison Building at the corner of Capitol and Market streets—just across the street from the State House—in June 1984. The move was not accomplished without casualties. "The loss of continuity, when some long-time senior staff persons were unable to move, was a predictable result," Quentin A. Blachly noted in his chairman's report early in 1985. "Additionally, the Executive Director resigned to accept a position in another state, the manager of Southwind was lost by death and previous Commission Chairman William S. Young decided to terminate his nine and one half years of outstanding leadership."[2] Blachly also reported to Governor Orr that the move to Indianapolis coincided with a planned enlargement of commission staff. During 1984, the Port Commission created positions for and hired a deputy executive director, marketing director, and rate specialist, all in Indianapolis, and a cargo representative at Burns Harbor.[3]

The Port Commission signified its intentions of moving in new directions by renaming its Lake Michigan port. At its August 27, 1984 meeting, commissioners adopted the name Port of Indiana/Burns International Harbor for the big lake port. "The new name more accurately reflects the international character of the vessels and cargoes serviced by the port and emphasizes the direct access to world markets which the port affords Indiana's shippers," noted the *Annual Report* for 1984.[4]

Beyond promotional and cosmetic changes, there were a number of major achievements at each of the ports during the 1980s. With thousands of acres of prime maritime industrial land for lease, the Port Commission concerned itself with its function as a landlord. Following the arrival of Frank G. Martin, Jr. as executive director, it adopted a formal Real Estate Brokers Compensation Policy to encourage industrial and economic development of port properties.[5]

The decade of the 1980s got off to a good start, symbolically

Frank G. Martin, Jr., executive director of the Indiana Port Commission, 1989 to present.

and substantively, on the occasion of the Port Commission's twentieth anniversary. Cargill, Inc., the giant grain trader and food processor based in Minneapolis, began operation of a $21,500,000 grain transfer facility at Burns International Harbor in June 1981. Appropriate ceremonies, attended by state, company, and Port Commission officials, marked the event, which was the beginning of a series of similar, but smaller-sized, projects announced for the three ports during the 1980s. At Burns International Harbor, new tenants early in the decade included Frick Farm Supply and Metro Metals, each of which handled enormous quantities of bulk cargo, including fertilizers, ores, and aggregates. Metro Metals Processing, Inc., which set up a facility at the port to engage in the tension leveling of steel, was a result of the combined economic development efforts of the Port Commission, the Indiana Department of Commerce, and the City of Portage. North American Towing Co., a tenant signed at the port in 1985, gave Burns International Harbor a second provider of tugboat and towing services.[6]

Indiana Port Commission Chairman William S. Young addressed guests at
the dedication of the Cargill grain export elevator at Burns Waterway
Harbor, August 1981. Seated (from left) are Cargill's Peter Kooi, Governor
Robert D. Orr, and Cargill's James Howard.

Stevedoring services at Burns International Harbor were provided
by several firms during the 1980s and 1990s. Ceres Marine Terminals, Inc., which had located at the port in 1975, was succeeded by
the Lakes and Rivers Transfer Corporation, one of the many road and
water transportation companies operated by local resident Jack Gray.
Lakes and Rivers, which continued to service the port as a stevedore
through 1995, became the primary tenant in the third large transit
shed erected by the Port Commission at Burns International Harbor
in 1989. Both Ceres and Lakes and Rivers had long experience providing stevedoring services to Great Lakes ports. Both stevedore companies established working relationships with the International Longshoremen's Association, which maintained an office at the port and
provided laborers to the companies through the union hiring hall. The
1980s were a time of tumultuous labor relations for most Great Lakes
ports; Ceres and Lakes and Rivers managed to maintain generally
harmonious and strike-free relations with the International Longshoreman's Association during that period.[7]

The *Canadoc*, a 600-foot laker, was the first ship to be loaded at the Cargill grain export facility at Burns Waterway Harbor in June 1981.

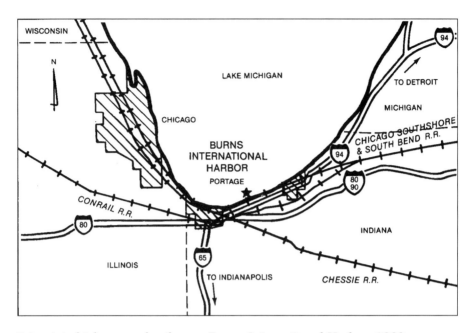

Interstate highway and rail map, Burns International Harbor, 1989.

Each of the river ports also attracted important new clients during the decade. Southwind built upon its auspicious beginning by also signing Cargill to a lease; the grain processing firm took over the lease and facilities of Triple T Corporation at the Mount Vernon port. Southwind also managed to land well-respected tenants like Hutson Company and MAPCO, INC., establishing a reputation for efficient handling of bulk grain, coal, and timber cargoes. By 1988, Southwind was handling more than 3,500,000 tons of cargo a year, over two-thirds of the total cargo shipped through the three state ports. Clark, just getting underway in 1985, already boasted of a steel processing plant, grain elevators, a stevedoring company, and several bulk storage pads in heavy use on its property. By 1988, Clark was handling over 500,000 tons of cargo a year, a respectable amount for what was essentially a start-up port. In July 1989, Clark signed a new tenant, Minerals Research and Recovery, Inc. of Tucson, Arizona, which shipped hematite (anhydrous ferric oxide, "widely used in the heavy appliance industry") from Canada, via Louisiana and by barge on the Mississippi and Ohio rivers, to Clark. The hematite was destined for use by manufacturers in Louisville and Evansville.[8]

The development of the river ports proved a boon to the state's farmers. William Uhrig, a professor of agricultural economics at

Attending the ribbon cutting in 1994 at the Hutson, Inc. 10,000-ton dry bulk fertilizer storage facility are (from left) Donald R. Snyder, port director, Southwind Maritime Centre; Indiana Port Commission Commissioner Arthur D. Hopkins; Port Commission Secretary-Treasurer N. Stuart Grauel; Hutson, Inc. Southwind Terminal Manager Wesley Harris; Port Commission Chairman William N. Kenefick; Hutson, Inc. Senior Vice President Marney Nunally; Port Commission Vice Chairman Norman E. Pfau, Jr.; and Port Commission Commissioners Marvin E. Ferguson and John D. Bottorff.

Purdue University, told the Indianapolis *News* in 1987 that the ports played an integral role in the state's economic infrastructure. The ports, he said, "are very important to the state's agricultural economy because they provide [a] low-cost transportation alternative. The state's grain export business has increased dramatically since the 1960s and we can point to the ports as one of the key reasons."[9]

After a relatively long period of stability, the 1980s were characterized by personnel changes, both among commissioners and administrative staff. Most administrative changes came in 1984, when the headquarters of the Port Commission was relocated from Burns Harbor to Indianapolis.

Six new commissioners were appointed during the 1980s. When Chairman Young retired in December 1983, he was replaced as chairman by eight-year-commission-veteran Quentin A. Blachly. Robert M. Schram, the Peru banker and farmer appointed as an original commissioner in 1961 by Governor Matthew E. Welsh, retired in 1983 after twenty-two years of dedicated service. Harry F. Zaklan, an Indianapolis municipal court judge, concluded nine years of service in 1985-1986. Governor Orr replaced all three men in 1985: Arthur D. Hopkins of Liberty, a marketing specialist formerly with the Indiana Department of Commerce; Robert L. Poor, a grain merchant from

Greencastle; and Joe E. Robertson, a well-traveled plywood manufacturer from Brownstown. Martin H. Gross, a businessman from Indianapolis, served for several months in 1985.[10]

Two more Port Commission appointments rounded out the 1980s. Incoming Governor Evan Bayh (1989-1997), whose victory at the polls in November 1988 marked the first time that the Democrats had captured the governor's office since 1965, had two appointments to make immediately. William E. Babinscak died in November 1988, and Chairman Blachly resigned early in 1989, after deviating from commission tradition by campaigning actively in Lake County for Republican John M. Mutz in the 1988 gubernatorial election. Bayh appointed R. Louie Gonzalez, an East Chicago educator and attorney, and William N. Kenefick, an attorney from Michigan City, to fill the two vacant slots on the Port Commission. William H. Keck from Mount Vernon, who had served on the commission since 1970, was elected chair. With these appointments, the political balance on the commission shifted in 1989, going to four Democrats and three Republicans. Hopkins, Pfau, and Poor were Republicans, and Robertson, Gonzalez, Keck, and Kenefick were Democrats.[11]

The chief executive officer of the Port Commission changed frequently during the 1980s. Following Jack P. Fitzgerald's departure in 1980, Ralph B. Joseph, formerly the Port Commission's director of operations, filled the office of port director. That title was later changed to executive director when each of the three ports was assigned a port director.

Joseph served as executive director for three years. He was succeeded in 1983 by James D. Pugh, who had served as Joseph's deputy director. Pugh left Indianapolis in 1984 for the Port of Houston, where he was eventually named executive director. He was replaced by Garth Whipple, a newspaper editor from Mount Vernon who had worked since 1980 in the Port Commission's marketing department. Whipple served as executive director until 1986. His successor was Robert D. Kraft, a former employee of the legal staff of the St. Lawrence Seaway Development Corporation. Kraft left in late 1988 for a lobbying position with the Indiana Farm Bureau and was replaced by Frank G. Martin, Jr.

Martin, a dedicated and aggressive administrator with experience at both the ports of Chicago and Coos Bay, Oregon, brought with him a dogged determination to make the Indiana ports even more competitive than they had already become. Martin quickly assembled a strong leadership team in Indianapolis and at the three ports. He kept the talented young port directors already in place—James D. Hartung

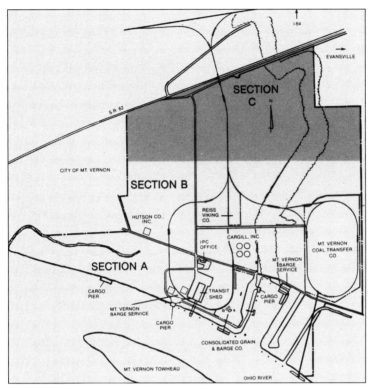

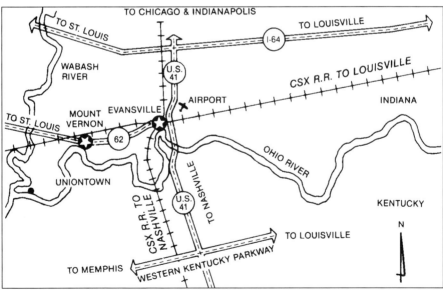

The site layout (top) and highway and rail map (bottom) for Southwind
Maritime Centre in 1986.

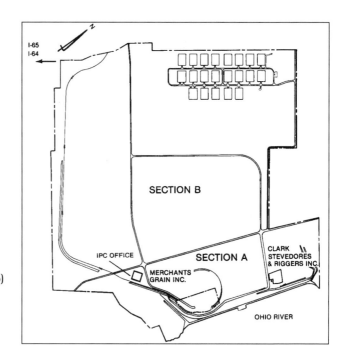

The site layout (top) and highway and rail map (bottom) for Clark Maritime Centre in 1986.

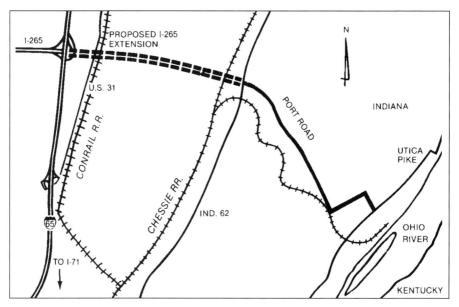

at Burns International Harbor and Chris V. Kinnett at Clark Maritime Centre—and added Donald R. Snyder, an experienced inland waterways executive, as the port director at Southwind Maritime Centre in 1989.

Martin brought John L. Coulter, a longtime trucking executive, out of retirement to serve as the new director of marketing. He also created the position of director of planning and grants, and filled it with William Friedman, a young graduate of the Indiana University School of Public and Environmental Affairs.[12] Martin also moved to strengthen the Port Commission's communications and finance functions.

The successful personnel changes were matched by promising market studies. Economic impact studies in 1983 by David G. Abraham of Quantum Research Corporation, noted that, "On the whole, it can be concluded that the State's investment in the two ports has been very fruitful to this point."[13]

The Port Commission and its administrators, however, faced a host of problems during the 1980s. Many of the problems were not unique to the ports of Indiana. They were dealt with by ports and commissions across the Great Lakes and the Ohio River Valley in varying degrees of severity. During the decade, however, there were a number of specific issues that adversely affected tonnages moving through Indiana's three public ports, in addition to the general sluggishness of the Midwest economy as a whole at the start of the decade and weather-related problems resulting in drought and low-water conditions for the region's inland waterways system at the decade's end.

The failure of the Valleyfield Bridge in Quebec on the St. Lawrence Seaway in 1984 contributed to the problems that bedeviled the Port Commission during the decade. In addition, the failure of the LaRoque Bridge near Montreal prevented at least eight foreign ships intending to call on Burns International Harbor from getting into the Great Lakes for the end of the season grain rush. As a result, Burns missed reaching, for the first time, the two-million-ton mark for a single year. Repair problems on the inland waterway system in Illinois also interrupted Burns Harbor barge service for three months during the same year.[14]

Difficulties of a bureaucratic nature prevented Public Law 480 cargo—agricultural shipments for humanitarian programs like Food for Peace—from using Indiana's lake port. Succumbing to pressure from maritime unions on the Atlantic and Gulf coasts, the U.S. Maritime Administration dictated that Public Law 480 cargo had to move in U.S. flag ships. Since the Great Lakes had little, if any, U.S. liner service, these ports were effectively shut out of bidding for Food for Peace cargoes. Even though Public Law 480 cargoes amounted to only

Port Director Donald R. Snyder (left) providing a tour of Southwind Maritime Centre in 1990 to U.S. Representative Frank McCloskey (D-Indiana).

two and one-half percent of the total tonnage handled at Burns in 1983, the labor intensive nature of the bagged shipments accounted for more than fifty percent of the International Longshoremen's Association man-hours worked at the port in 1983. When Great Lakes congressmen finally managed to convince the Maritime Administration to establish a set-aside program for Food for Peace shipments in the lakes, the railroads diverted most bagged commodities shipments to ports on the Atlantic and Gulf coasts. Long negotiations and a lawsuit finally paved the way for Public Law 480 cargoes to be handled at Burns International Harbor.[15]

The expensive and ultimately futile litigation with Bethlehem Steel over harbor service charges dragged on throughout much of the decade and was finally abandoned by the Port Commission in 1988. Also in litigation during the decade were disputes over payments for dock wall and ship damage during 1984 storms, a disagreement with Ceres Marine Terminals involving fees owed by the former tenant, and a suit filed by Ogden Dunes residents west of Burns International Harbor regarding erosion and other environmental damages to the lakeshore allegedly caused by nearby port structures.[16] These problems, however, were relatively minor.

A potentially troublesome policy reform of the 1980s involved the continued independence of the Port Commission. In 1978, the Indiana General Assembly enacted "sunset" legislation. The Port Commission was included in the law under the functional category of Highway or Transportation Matters. The published audit, required by the legislation, only makes observations and recommendations about funding. The possibility of the Port Commission becoming a unit within the Indiana Department of Transportation, however, was viewed favorably by some state policymakers as the 1980s began. The Port Commission was able to persuade state authorities in 1980 that its unique status as a quasi-independent agency, operating on business rather than political principles should be preserved. Among other reasons, the commission pointed out that the need for quick response to business conditions required its separate standing.[17]

The Port Commission ended the 1980s in good shape, buoyed by a resurgent Midwest economy. Steel, grain, and coal—commodities handled by all three public ports—rebounded sharply from the recession earlier in the decade. The commission had good reason to look forward to ever improving business conditions in the 1990s.

Bagged grain foodstuffs, bound for India as part of the Public Law 480 Food for Peace Program, being loaded at Burns International Harbor in 1984.

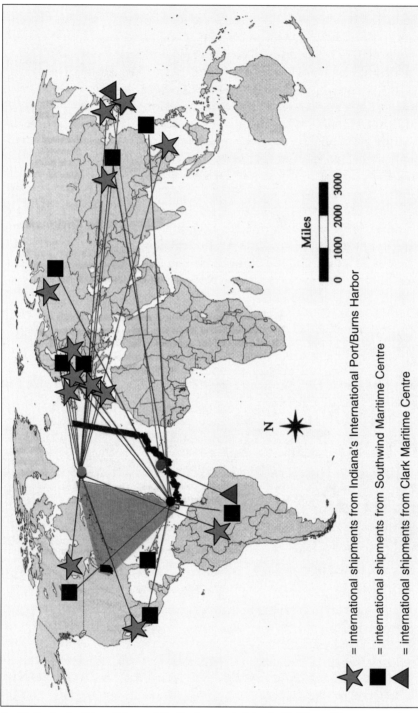

International shipments through the international public ports of Indiana, 1994.

= international shipments from Indiana's International Port/Burns Harbor

= international shipments from Southwind Maritime Centre

= international shipments from Clark Maritime Centre

Miles

0    1000  2000  3000

N

Credit: Center for Urban Policy and the Environment, School of Public and Environmental
Affairs, Indiana University.

# EPILOGUE

# The Indiana Port Commission
# in the 1990s

*by Bill Beck*

The three ports operated by the Indiana Port Commission enjoyed record tonnages in 1994, fueled partly by a flood of imported iron and steel products and the continuing strong rebound of Indiana's economy.

Clark Maritime Centre at Jeffersonville reported tonnage of more than 1,450,000 tons, up four percent from the 1,400,000 tons reported in 1993. Steel rods and coils, gypsum, salt, and lightweight aggregate all showed significant tonnage increase. A total of 971 barges were handled at Clark, up eight percent from 1993. Clark reported total revenues of $217,800, a $27,000 jump from 1993. In the summer of 1994, Clark celebrated the opening of Interstate 265 to the port.

Southwind Maritime Centre at Mount Vernon handled total tonnage of just over 5,000,000 tons, up three percent from the record 4,925,000 tons reported in 1993. Revenues for 1994 were almost $595,000, up twelve percent over the nearly $530,000 in 1993. The Ohio River port reported increased tonnage of inbound cargoes, including pig iron and precious metals. Outbound cargo, which consists primarily of coal, grain, and logs, was down slightly from the 4,500,000 tons handled in 1993. The port ended the year handling 2,354 barges, up six percent from the 2,231 barges handled in 1993.

Semi-finished steel slabs propelled Indiana's International Port at Burns Harbor to a record-shattering year. The big port on Lake Michigan in Porter County handled 3,095,133 tons of cargo in 1994, up a whopping thirty-five percent from the 2,300,000 tons of cargo handled in 1993. Almost half of the International Port's record tonnage—1,430,000 tons—came in the form of import semi-finished steel slabs destined for the integrated steel mills that call northwestern Indiana home. Other steel cargo included steel coils, steel beams, steel sheets, and steel plates.[1]

By the mid-1990s, Indiana policymakers understood more fully the critical role that Indiana's public ports played in economic development in the state. Indiana's three ports are "critically important economic assets for Hoosier families, the state of Indiana, and the Midwest," reported a study published in July 1994 by the Center for Urban Policy and the Environment, Indiana University. The center again studied the economic impacts of the three ports in 1996 and issued an updated report in January 1997. The initial findings exceeded the commission's expectations.[2]

The ports generate at least $326,000,000 in economic impact for Indiana and $500,000,000 of impact across the states of Indiana, Illinois, and Kentucky, researchers found. *The Ports of the Indiana Port Commission: Economic Impacts and Economic Development,* issued in 1994, was the first comprehensive study of Indiana's International Port at Burns Harbor, Southwind Maritime Centre, and Clark Maritime Centre to examine fully the ports' effects on the Indiana economy.

The ports are responsible for 3,577 jobs in Indiana, generating almost $93,000,000 in salaries and benefits for Hoosier families. That total includes nearly 1,550 direct jobs and another more than 2,000 indirect jobs created by the three ports. The three ports pay more than $5,750,000 in state taxes each year. The gross assessed value of property at the ports was more than $30,000,000 in 1993—the initial study year—and that generated $1,800,000 in local taxes.

Indiana's public ports attracted a substantial level of private investment. In 1992 and 1993, private firms invested more than $120,000,000 in facilities located at the ports. For every dollar invested by the public sector in Indiana's three ports, the private sector invested $6.93.[3]

Keeping the ports maintained and in top-working order is an expensive and time-consuming task. An innovative joint Indiana Port Commission/U.S. Army Corps of Engineers project at Indiana's International Port at Burns Harbor is resulting in a major reconstruction of the existing breakwater and construction of a new underwater segmented reef that will reduce wave force on the existing breakwater.

The $13,000,000 project got underway in June 1995 and is expected to be completed by 1998. The construction of the $10,900,000 underwater segmented reef is designed to eliminate wave action within the harbor and to provide sand for the nourishment of the public beach at Ogden Dunes.

Governor Evan Bayh (1989-1997) paid tribute to the aggressive efforts of Indiana's congressional delegates, "particularly Congressman Pete Visclosky and John Myers, who authored this legislation and appropriation over a four-year period in the U.S. Congress."

The on-going project involves three phases, including dredging, reconstruction of the breakwater, and construction of the underwater segmented reef. Approximately 300,000 cubic yards of material were removed during the dredging phase of the project. The dredging helps maintain the existing thirty-foot-deep shipping channel.

Approximately 70,000 cubic yards of the dredged material, which consists primarily of clean sand, will be piped to the adjacent beach at Ogden Dunes for the purpose of beach nourishment.[4]

On June 26, 1995, the Port Commission dedicated two projects at Southwind Maritime Centre at Mount Vernon that would solidify the Ohio River port's reputation as one of the most cost-efficient dock facilities on America's inland waterways.

Commissioners dedicated an enhanced rail project and a major expansion of the Foreign Trade Zone (FTZ) at Southwind. The projects would contribute to Southwind's growing ability to meet the shipping needs of customers in southern Indiana, northern Kentucky, and southeastern Illinois.

The rail enhancement project added an additional 2,000 feet of line to Southwind's short line rail system. It enabled the port to handle recent increases in the movement of high-dollar commodities such as coal, pig iron, and steel, and to accommodate increasing cargo volume anticipated in future years.

Southwind's FTZ, a vital tool in the enticement of international trade and development to the port, was expanded to twenty-one acres. The commission had long been a champion of FTZs, which allows shippers and manufacturers to store import and export parts and components duty-free. The expanded FTZ encompassed a state-of-the-art, 58,000-square-foot transit shed equipped with a sixty-ton bridge crane for more efficient cargo handling.[5]

Credit: Indiana State Archives.

"Indiana's International Port is one of the premier ports on the Great Lakes and is one of the main reasons we have been able to attract solid companies with good family-wage jobs to Indiana. . . . the Lake Michigan port is the crown jewel of the Great Lakes."

*Evan Bayh*
*June 29, 1995*
*Governor of Indiana, 1989-1997*

Several days later, on June 29, 1995, Governor Bayh was at Indiana's International Port to announce economic development initiatives that would support expansion of three projects at the Lake Michigan port.

Describing the International Port as the "crown jewel of the Great Lakes," Governor Bayh recognized the efforts toward the planning of a $40,000,000 joint venture steel mill for the port; the opening of a steel servicing center by Steel Warehouse of South Bend; and the start-up of a competitive tug service at the port by Eagle Marine Towing Co. of Gary.[6]

Meanwhile, an editorial appeared in the Indianapolis *Star* concerning the surge in the demand for steel and its effect on Indiana's International Port. The editorial noted that "mills in the northwestern part of the state account for about one-fourth of the nation's annual production of steel." It also pointed out that increased demand abroad due to the growing economic strength of Europe and Asia, coupled with the decline in the value of the dollar, accounted for much of the surge in steel exports. The editorial went on to cite heightened interest in the International Port, including planned construction of a $40,000,000 minimill for Chicago Cold Rolling Corp., construction of a $1,200,000 FTZ warehouse, and the building of a $600,000 warehouse for storing hot-rolled steel at the port. "The glory days are gone and no one expects them to return," stated the editorial. "But it's a safe bet that steel will do more to revive the prospects of northern Indiana than any floating casino ever will."[7]

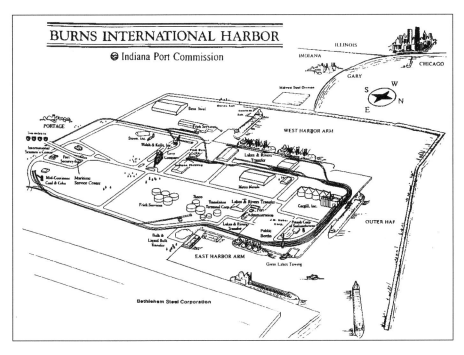

Burns International Harbor in the early 1990s; sketch of a bird's-eye-view looking southwest.

Economic development was not constrained to the International Port. In February 1996, Chemtrusion, a plastics firm based in Houston, Texas, broke ground for a new multi-million dollar thermoplastics compounding facility at Clark Maritime Centre at Jeffersonville. The firm had announced the previous November that it would build the new $12,500,000 facility on a fifteen-acre site at the Ohio River port.

Chemtrusion announced it would compound thermal plastic resins at the 170,000-square-foot facility, providing seventy-six new jobs to the area. The plant would supply the automotive manufacturing industry in Indiana and the lower Midwest. Chemtrusion and its partner, Mytex Polymers, a joint venture of Mitsubishi Chemical Inc. and Exxon Chemical Inc., planned to have the new facility in full operation by late 1996. Chemtrusion is a subsidiary of Intersystem Inc. of Houston, Texas.[8]

The Indiana Department of Commerce, headed by Lieutenant Governor Frank L. O'Bannon (1989-1997), assisted Chemtrusion with an infrastructure grant to Jeffersonville for $284,000 and a $20,000 grant to train new workers.[9]

In March 1996, the Port Commission approved a master plan for Indiana's International Port that would help guide the Lake Michigan port through the turn of the twenty-first century and beyond.

The master plan set guidelines for maximizing use of existing facilities and for maximizing flexibility of tenant use. The plan also would accomplish a number of other goals, including maintaining and improving efficiency of materials-handling facilities; enhancing intermodal access; reinforcing the ability to handle diverse cargoes; organizing land-use patterns; and prioritizing land use by revenue generation within the port. The plan laid the groundwork for the continued growth and expansion of the port by improving and extending the port's existing infrastructure. The International Port had evolved from a niche port specializing in bulk cargo to an international port with an ever-increasing emphasis on processing.[10]

The news also continued to be good for the Ohio River ports. Clark Maritime Centre reached a coveted milestone in mid-February 1996. The Ohio River port near Jeffersonville recorded its ten millionth ton of general cargo. Clark handles steel rods, steel coils, scrap steel, paper, hardboard, corn, soybeans, wheat, oats, salt, fertilizer, sand, aggregate, machinery, concrete, logs, pig iron, gypsum, and glass. In 1995, the port handled just over 1,300,000 tons of cargo, slightly below the record set in 1994. Clark began operations in 1985 and had moved an average of just under 1,000,000 tons of cargo a year during its operational history. But the rapid expansion of the port's tenant base after 1990 contributed to a strong demand for river shipping.[11]

Voss Clark, a steel processing company located at Clark Maritime Centre, in the spring of 1996 announced plans for a $5,300,000 expansion at its two-and-one-half-year-old facility. The expansion involved purchasing new equipment, hiring ten additional workers, and adding an undetermined addition to the 225,000-square-foot plant. At the time, the plant employed fifty-two people. Approximately 400,000 tons of steel were processed a year by Voss Clark at the Ohio River port facility for use in automobile and appliance manufacturing. Voss Clark used the port to transport steel by barge, rail, and truck.[12]

But the real economic development action in Indiana was happening in the southwestern corner of the state. Toyota's announcement early in 1996 that it would build a pickup truck assembly plant in Gibson County, and AK Steel's late 1996 announcement of the construction of a steel finishing mill near Rockport were two of the biggest economic development projects of the decade in the state.

By the summer of 1996, Southwind Maritime Centre at Mount Vernon appeared to be the location of choice for Midwest soybean processors. Two big grain firms in recent months had chosen the Ohio River port as the site for major new soybean processing facilities.

ConAgra Trading and Processing Company, based in Omaha, Nebraska, announced in late July that it intended to invest nearly $170,000,000 to build a fully integrated soybean crushing, refining, and packaging complex at Southwind.

ConAgra's announcement followed the December 1995 announcement by CGB Enterprises Inc. that it intended to build a $25,000,000 soybean processing plant at Southwind. The firm, whose wholly owned subsidiary Consolidated Grain & Barge was a longtime port tenant, was based in Mandeville, Louisiana and had already committed $7,000,000 in equipment and engineering costs to the Southwind location.

ConAgra planned to begin construction in late 1996, with completion scheduled for the spring of 1998. Located on eighty-five acres, the complex's buildings would occupy more than 200,000 square feet, including twelve grain elevators.

ConAgra anticipated that it would purchase close to 50,000,000 bushels of soybeans a year, much of that from Indiana farmers, in order to supply the facility. That amount represented 2,800,000 tons per year of inbound and outbound freight to be shipped by rail, barge, and truck.[13]

"ConAgra's decision to locate here will have a broader economic impact than what is apparent on the surface," Governor Evan Bayh said in welcoming the international grain firm to Southwind. "ConAgra's choice will have a significant effect on Indiana's agribusiness, on our Southwind port operations and on Hoosier businesses engaged in transport."[14]

Personnel matters have been relatively stable during this decade, at least on the administrative side. Frank G. Martin, Jr. has continued to build an outstanding administrative team in Indianapolis and at the three ports. James D. Hartung, the talented port director at Burns International Harbor, left Indiana in 1993 for a position as head of Toledo's port and airport authority. Hartung was replaced by

E. Peter McCarthy, a twenty-five-year maritime veteran who had been Hartung's deputy port director. John L. Coulter took a second retirement in 1993, and Martin restructured the position to handle both communications and marketing. Warren J. Brodine, an Indiana University graduate, filled the position from 1993 to 1995. He was replaced by Don W. Miller, Jr., a native of Kentucky. He had served as director of marketing for the Port of Brookings, Oregon, and was a congressional legislative assistant before joining the Port Commission. Miller grew up in Oregon and received a B.S. degree from the University of Oregon. Port planning director William Friedman left the Port Commission in 1991, and was replaced by William Fritchley, a retired U.S. Army officer.

Chris V. Kinnett, longtime port director of Clark Maritime Centre, left the port in September 1996 to become head of the Vincennes Area Community Development Corporation in Vincennes, Indiana. Port Commission Chairman N. Stuart Grauel described Kinnett as "essentially responsible for building Clark Maritime Centre from the ground up." Kinnett had joined the staff of the Port Commission in 1984 as port director at Southwind Maritime Centre at Mount Vernon. From 1985 to 1988, Kinnett served as port director at both Southwind and the newly opened Clark Maritime Centre. In early 1989, Donald R. Snyder was named port director at Southwind, and Kinnett took responsibility for cargo and industrial development at Clark. During his tenure, Kinnett compiled an outstanding industrial development record and saw Clark record its ten millionth ton of cargo.[15]

Kinnett's departure occasioned other changes in the Port Commission staff. Don W. Miller, Jr. was named port director at Clark Maritime Centre in Jeffersonville, replacing Kinnett. Miller assumed his duties at the Ohio River port February 1, 1997. Replacing Miller as director of communications was Spencer Valentine. Raised in Fort Wayne, Indiana, Valentine earned a B.S. degree at Ball State University in Muncie. Prior to joining the Port Commission staff, Valentine worked for the Indiana General Assembly, the Indiana Department of Commerce, and the Indiana Housing Finance Authority.[16]

There was a major turnover in Port Commission commissioners under the administration of Governor Evan Bayh. The entire commission was replaced between 1991 and 1995. Governor Bayh, therefore, appointed seven commissioners in a little over four years, the most commissioners appointed in such a short period of time since Governor Welsh appointed the original commissioners in 1961.

N. Stuart Grauel, vice president for public affairs at IPALCO

**"There have been a number of high points during the seven years I've served on the Indiana Port Commission. In fact, two of them—one general and one specific—finished neck and neck. For me, it's a tie between seeing the two Ohio River ports finally blossom, and, at the same time, seeing the efforts of the Commission and Federal Marine rewarded by the arrival of regular liner service at the International Port."**

_N. Stuart Grauel_
_October 1997_
_Indiana Port Commission_
_commissioner, 1991-current,_
_and chairman, 1995-current_

Enterprises, the holding company for Indianapolis Power & Light Company, was appointed in February 1991 and reappointed in July 1994; Grauel became Port Commission chairman after William N. Kenefick's death in August 1995. John D. Bottorff, president and CEO of the Seymour Chamber of Commerce and Indiana Secretary of State from 1964 to 1966, was appointed in October 1991 and reappointed in July 1995. Marvin E. Ferguson, founder and chairman emeritus of Ferguson Steel Company in Indianapolis and a former commissioner of the Indiana Alcoholic Beverage Commission, was appointed in September 1993 and reappointed in July 1994. W. Ken Massengill of East Chicago, Indiana Steelworkers Political Education Committee legislative director and employed by the United Steelworkers of America since 1974, was appointed in January 1994. Steven E. Chancellor, former chairman, chief executive officer, and president of Black Beauty Coal Co., Evansville, and a member of the University of Southern Indiana Foundation board of directors, was appointed in July 1994. Mary Ann Fagan, an Indianapolis homemaker, who spent nearly a decade in the insurance industry and then became active in

"What sets me apart is that I was the first female appointed to the Commission. And to tell the truth, before I was appointed, I didn't really know we had three ports in Indiana or that we provided as many jobs as we do or that the ports are as well-managed as they are. I can remember, right after my appointment, attending a fiftieth wedding anniversary for my in-laws and trying to explain to my father-in-law that it was the PORT Commission, and not 'the other white meat.'"

*Mary Ann Fagan*
*October 1997*
*Indiana Port Commission*
*commissioner, 1995-current*

the volunteer sector, was appointed in July 1995 and is the first woman to serve as a commissioner. Joseph E. Costanza, an attorney in private practice in Ogden Dunes and past president of the East Chicago Chamber of Commerce, was appointed in October 1995.

Another personnel change came early in the administration of Governor Frank L. O'Bannon (1997-). The resignation of Steven Chancellor from the commission opened the way for O'Bannon to make his first appointment to the seven-member commission, longtime Hoosier business leader H. C. "Bud" Farmer, former president and chairman of the board of Evansville Concrete Corp. Farmer, of Evansville, graduated from the University of Evansville and was a thirty-year veteran of southwestern Indiana's concrete industry. His numerous civic memberships reflect his lifelong commitment to economic development and his keen interest in the state's public ports.[17]

New construction at the International Port kept alive the memory of one of the ports' staunchest friends. The William N. Kenefick Adminis-

William N. Kenefick, an Indiana Port Commission commissioner, 1989-1995, and chairman, 1993-1995.

tration Building at Indiana's International Port was dedicated on November 12, 1996. The new 8,400-square-foot facility replaced a twenty-six-year-old relic of a building that formerly housed port administration staffers.[18]

Kenefick died in Michigan City at the age of eighty-three on August 10, 1995. A Port Commission member from 1989 to 1995, Kenefick served as commission chairman from 1993 to 1995. Kenefick was a lifelong resident of Michigan City and a third generation practicing attorney. A well-known land developer in northern Indiana, his visionary leadership was instrumental in the development of many civic and community projects.[19]

The Kenefick Administration Building is a steel-studded building, constructed with steel beams rather than wooden two-by-fours. "America's Steel Port" wanted to demonstrate continuing support for the region's steel industry.[20]

The January 1997 port economic impact study—*The Ports of the Indiana Port Commission: Economic Impacts and Economic Development*—revealed the good news that Indiana's three public ports not only served as a vital transportation network for the state, but also contributed to the economic development of various local communities and had a substantial economic impact on the state as a whole.[21]

The study, conducted by the Center for Urban Policy and the Environment, Indiana University, found that the most important port impact in 1995 was an annual output of $587,000,000, produced by workers in 5,771 jobs throughout the state. Of this total, Indiana's International Port was responsible for $409,000,000 and 3,730 jobs; Southwind Maritime Centre accounted for $70,000,000 and 838 jobs; and Clark Maritime Centre made up $108,000,000 and 1,203 jobs.[22]

*The Ports of the Indiana Port Commission* detailed the three ports' substantial tax contribution in 1995. The ports paid more than $12,000,000 in Indiana state and local taxes; $9,000,000 of that was generated by state tax revenue, including such taxes as the personal income tax of employees, corporate income taxes from tenant industries, sales tax, and motor fuel tax. The remaining $3,000,000 was applied toward property taxes, the majority going to Clark, Porter, and Posey counties where the ports are located.[23]

In recent years, all three ports had posted consistently positive net revenues. Indiana's International Port had shown positive annual net revenues since 1986, with the exception of 1990. Southwind also had posted positive net revenues annually, while Clark continued to show positive net revenues throughout the mid-1990s. After covering operating costs, a substantial portion of the surplus was invested in port infrastructure, such as rail, road, dock, and bridge improvements.

The positive revenues helped to keep the Port Commission one of a handful in the nation that relied on their own revenues for operating expenses rather than tax dollars. Sources included primarily revenue from rent, leases, and other fees paid by tenant firms as well as revenue from general maritime activity. Administration of FTZs also yielded a small but important revenue contribution annually.[24]

Researchers noted that the private sector invested $8.82 for every dollar invested by state and local government. "Indiana's public ports are a critical asset to Indiana's economic and transportation base," the study concluded.[25]

Expansion at Indiana's International Port continued. The steel producer Feralloy Corporation, based in Chicago, on November 1, 1996, broke ground for a major expansion at Indiana's International Port. The new 187,000-square-foot facility would join two facilities already at the port in which Feralloy had an interest.

Port and local officials at the groundbreaking joined Feralloy President Frank M. Walker and Ken L. Sterbenz, general manager of Feralloy's Midwest Division. Lieutenant Governor Frank L. O'Bannon, who would win his election to the governor's office just three days later, attended as guest of honor.

The $20,000,000 plant would have its own processing and distribution center for shipping and receiving steel by truck, rail, barge, and ocean vessel. Port Commission officials estimated the new facility would add about 100,000 tons of new cargo annually for the Lake Michigan port.

The new facility would create jobs for about 100 production workers and employ an office staff of ten people. Lieutenant Governor O'Bannon promised the state's assistance by committing a $70,000 Department of Commerce grant for workforce training.[26]

Even better news for the future of the International Port came late in 1996. FedNav, one of the premier shipping companies on the Great Lakes/St. Lawrence Seaway system, announced plans to begin providing stevedoring and scheduled liner service to Indiana's International Port.[27]

Indiana Stevedoring and Distribution Corporation (ISD), which is an equally owned joint venture of FedNav Limited of Montreal, Quebec and Alternative Distribution Systems, Inc. (ADS) of Homewood, Illinois, announced the multi-year agreement with the Port Commission. ISD had been negotiating a lease with the commission since the summer of 1996.[28] Beginning January 1, 1999, ISD would provide services as a general cargo terminal operator and stevedore at Indiana's International Port. By mid-1997, ISD would contract with Roll & Hold Warehousing & Distribution to build and begin operating a metals warehouse and distribution center at the port.[29] A second phase of construction to expand the center was scheduled for completion in 1999.

The agreement also provided for FedNav to relocate its cargo-handling operations and steamship service to Indiana's International Port from the nearby Port of Chicago effective January 1999. The relocation of Federal Atlantic Lakes Line (FALLINE), the largest dedicated liner service operating between Europe and the Great Lakes, would be the first time in the port's history that a dedicated liner service would be offered on a regularly scheduled basis.[30]

With the increasing movement of import semi-finished steel slabs through the international port, FedNav looked to be making a good bet in moving from Chicago. In the spring of 1997, Indiana's International Port on Lake Michigan anticipated one of its best years ever, as it handled imported semi-finished slabs for neighboring integrated mills in northwestern Indiana. At the same time, Clark Maritime Centre on the Ohio River was handling more and more steel as tenant steel processors and distributors like Voss Clark and Wayne Steel increased their business.

In 1995, Indiana's International Port handled 3,000,000 tons of maritime cargo. Tonnages dropped off in 1996 to 2,400,000 tons, but observers of the domestic steel industry expected 1997 to be a banner year for steel imports into the Great Lakes' ports.

The opening of the new Chicago Cold Rolling Corp. facility and

Feralloy's new plant at Indiana's International Port were expected to increase the demand for steel products at the port.

Experts predicted that imported semi-finished steel ingots, billets, blooms, and slabs could reach twenty-six percent of the nation's steel imports in 1997. In the record year of 1995, semi-finished steel products had accounted for one-quarter of the nation's slightly more than 30,000,000 tons of steel imports.

The United States imported 38,300,000 tons of iron and steel products in 1996, a 24.3 percent increase over 1995 and the highest volume handled in the last four years.[31]

The worst floods on the Ohio River in a generation struck Clark Maritime Centre and Southwind Maritime Centre in March 1997. But the floods were unable to halt operations at the two river ports, largely because the Port Commission had planned and developed the facilities above the 100-year flood plain.

The flooding in the first week of March was brought about by torrential rains in the Ohio River basin the previous weekend. On March 5, the river crested thirteen feet above the twenty-three-foot flood stage at Jeffersonville, lapping less than eight inches from the warehouse of American Commercial Marine Service Company (ACMS), the port's general cargo stevedore.

Clark Maritime Centre transloaded steel trucks throughout the flooding, with every business at the port open and operating. The U.S. Army Corps of Engineers, however, closed the river at Jeffersonville to barge traffic for nearly a week.

The flood crest rolled downstream and threatened Southwind Maritime Centre in mid-March. While Piers One, Two, and Three were unable to operate for about ten days, the craneway at the Mount Vernon port loaded coal throughout the flood. Rail and truck service also continued.[32]

The U.S. Army Corps of Engineers has continued to improve the infrastructure of the Ohio River. Significant to the river ports during this decade has been the anticipated completion of a $2,500,000,000 renovation of the locks and dams along the Ohio River and its tributaries. Groundbreaking on a $299,700,000 reconstruction of the McAlpine Lock and Dam on the Ohio River at Louisville took place during the spring of 1996, and additional improvements are slated for Uniontown, Newburgh, and Cannelton before the turn of the century. Completion of the twenty-year project to upgrade the river's navigation channel will make the Ohio a "'state-of-the-art' waterway system 'unparalleled anywhere else in the world.'"[33]

In May 1997, the Indiana Port Commission helped honor retired Congressman John T. Myers, one of the strongest advocates of Indiana's Ohio River public port system. On May 9, the corps dedicated the John T. Myers Locks and Dam near Uniontown, Kentucky, just upstream from the confluence of the Wabash and Ohio rivers.[34]

With more tonnage than transits the Panama Canal moving down the Ohio River each year past Clark Maritime Centre at Jeffersonville and Southwind Maritime Centre at Mount Vernon, and with ever increasing volumes of import and export steel moving across the docks at Indiana's International Port/Burns Harbor at Portage, the future for Indiana's public port system is bright indeed.[35]

## Chapter 1, Waterways in Indiana History

[1] Clarence Edwin Carter, ed., *The Territorial Papers of the United States* (28 vols., Washington, D.C.: U.S. Government Printing Office, 1933-1950), 2:48. For the complete text of the ordinance, as well as a thorough analysis of the document, see Robert M. Taylor, Jr., ed., *The Northwest Ordinance: A Bicentennial Handbook* (Indianapolis: Indiana Historical Society, 1987).

[2] Chapter 57, *Acts Passed at the First Session of the Fourteenth Congress of the United States* (1817), 59. A copy of the Enabling Act is included in Hubert H. Hawkins, comp., *Indiana's Road to Statehood: A Documentary Record* (Indianapolis: Indiana Historical Bureau, 1969), 64-67. See also Volume 1 of Charles Kettleborough, *Constitution Making in Indiana* (4 vols., Indianapolis: Indiana Historical Bureau, 1916-1978), for documents relating to the boundaries of Indiana. The Indiana boundary question is discussed in Mrs. Frank J. Sheehan, *The Northern Boundary of Indiana* (Indianapolis: Indiana Historical Society, 1928). Ohio and Michigan also had a boundary dispute, known as the "Toledo War." For a complete discussion, see R. Carlyle Buley, *The Old Northwest: Pioneer Period, 1815-1840* (2 vols., Indianapolis: Indiana Historical Society, 1950), 2:190-203. Jennings soon became the first governor (1816-1822) of the state of Indiana.

[3] The best general history of the American canal system is in George Rogers Taylor, *The Transportation Revolution, 1815-1860* (New York: Harper & Row, 1951), 32-55. See also Ronald E. Shaw, *Canals for a Nation: The Canal Era in the United States, 1790-1860* (Lexington: The University Press of Kentucky, 1990). For Indiana specifically, see Paul Fatout, *Indiana Canals* (West Lafayette: Purdue University Studies, 1972).

[4] Port Commerce, founded by J. M. H. and John F. Allison to capitalize on canal linkage, was located to the east of the junction of the Eel and White rivers, across from Worthington. Robert M. Taylor, Jr. *et al.*, *Indiana: A New Historical Guide* (Indianapolis: Indiana Historical Society, 1989), 345-46; *Illustrated Historical Atlas . . .* (Chicago: Baskin, Forster & Co., 1876), 155.

[5] For an extensive discussion of this topic, see Ralph D. Gray, "The Canal Era in Indiana," in *Transportation and the Early Nation* (Indianapolis: Indiana Historical Society, 1982), 113-34. In 1836, the state had adopted improvements estimated to cost in excess of $10,000,000, borrowed at five percent interest; the annual state revenue was approximately $75,000. As a result of the state's financial crisis beginning in the late 1830s because of mismanagement of various internal improvements projects, a section prohibiting the state from going into debt was placed in the Constitution of 1851. James H. Madison, *The Indiana Way: A State History* (Bloomington: Indiana University Press, 1986), 82-86.

[6] Gray, "The Canal Era in Indiana," 126-27.

[7] DeWitt Clinton, an avid supporter of the Erie Canal, was mayor of New York from 1803 to 1815 (except terms 1807-1808 and 1810-1811) and governor of New York from 1817 to 1822. *Concise Dictionary of American Biography* (New York: Charles Scribner's Sons, 1977), 183-84.

[8] The station was designed by Joseph Curzon and located just south of the present Union Station. It served five tracks. It was enlarged in 1866 and demolished in 1886. David J. Bodenhamer and Robert G. Barrows, eds., *The Encyclopedia of Indianapolis* (Bloomington: Indiana University Press, 1994), 1363.

[9] Gilbert C. Fite and Jim E. Reese, *An Economic History of the United States* (2nd ed., Boston: Houghton Mifflin Company, 1965), 343.

[10] *Ibid.*, 343, 344. Ton-mileage is determined by multiplying a shipment's weight by the total number of miles it is transported. It is a unit of measurement used in both water and land transportation.

[11] Robert A. Hahn, *The Ohio River Basin Navigation System: 1988 Report* (Cincinnati: U.S. Army Corps of Engineers, Ohio River Division, 1988), 16. The United States Army Corps of Engineers was established in 1802 during the administration of President Thomas Jefferson (1801-1809).

**Chapter 2, Developments in Northwest Indiana**

[1] The introductory material is based on Robert M. Taylor, Jr. *et al., Indiana: A New Historical Guide* (Indianapolis: Indiana Historical Society, 1989), 573-76. The standard history of this area is Powell A. Moore, *The Calumet Region: Indiana's Last Frontier* (Indianapolis: Indiana Historical Bureau, 1959, reprint 1991).

[2] Nellie Armstrong Robertson and Dorothy Riker, eds., *The John Tipton Papers* (3 vols., Indianapolis: Indiana Historical Bureau, 1942), 1:271.

[3] Taylor *et al., Indiana,* 574-76; see *The New Encyclopedia Britannica* (Chicago: Encyclopedia Britannica, Inc., 1990), 12:216, regarding United States Steel.

[4] Gary *Post-Tribune,* September 25, 1925, August 6, 1926. Moore, *Calumet Region,* 12-13; Brigadier General G. B. Pillsbury, Corps of Engineers, U.S. War Department, Board of Engineers for Rivers and Harbors, "Subject: Burns Ditch Harbor, Indiana," March 16, 1936, Indiana Port Commission Files, Indiana State Archives. The case, *Lake Shore and Michigan Southern Railway Company et al.* v. *Clough et al.,* was filed in the Porter County Circuit Court. The Indiana Supreme Court denied rehearing on July 3, 1914, 182 Ind. 178. The case was appealed up the line: 104 N.E. 975, 105 N.E. 905, 242 U.S. 375. The U.S. Supreme Court affirmed the original judgment, hearing the case on November 9-10, 1916 and deciding it on January 8, 1917, 37 *Supreme Court Reporter* 144.

[5] *Yearbook of the State of Indiana for the Year 1920* (Indianapolis, 1921), 299-301, quotations, 299, 300. The state parks, dating from 1916, were operated by the Division of Lands and Waters which became part of the Department of Conservation in 1919. Indiana *Laws,* 1919, pp. 375, 385, and *Yearbook of the State of Indiana for the Year 1919* (Indianapolis, 1920), 370-76, 439-41. Lieber, first director of the Department of Conservation, is generally recognized as the "father of the Indiana state parks." Clifton J. Phillips, *Indiana in Transition: The Emergence of an Industrial Commonwealth, 1880-1920* (Indianapolis: Indiana Historical Bureau and Indiana Historical Society, 1968), 220-23.

[6] *Yearbook of the State of Indiana for the Year 1925* (Indianapolis, 1926), 400-3; Indiana *Laws,* 1921, special session, 266-68.

[7] At one time Nelson planned to write a history of the port and the Port

Commission. He collected voluminous records, but eventually he had to abandon his plans. He did, however, donate some extraordinarily valuable files, including personal correspondence, photographs, newspaper clippings, and various published reports, to the Indiana State Library in Indianapolis. The unprocessed Nelson files are now housed in the Indiana State Archives. The Indiana State Library has a transcript of an interview with Nelson recorded in 1976 and 1977. Although some aspects of the nineteenth-century background as related by Nelson are erroneous, his inside information regarding developments in the twentieth century is invaluable. See George Andrew Nelson Oral History Interview Transcript, 1983, Oral History Project, Indiana Division, Indiana State Library.

One example of erroneous information—that seems to have become folklore—is the assertion by Nelson and others associated with the port that Daniel Webster was interested in an Indiana port near Michigan City in 1832. In fact, Webster did not come to Indiana until 1837 as part of a multi-state tour. See, for example, Indianapolis *Journal,* June 17, 1837.

Nelson, an original member of the Indiana Port Commission whose memory is perpetuated in the name of the main road into Indiana's International Port, was clearly the key person in the long struggle to get an Indiana lakeport. Nelson worked on this project from the time he arrived in Valparaiso in the early 1930s until its realization in the 1960s, and he served on the Port Commission during its critical first fifteen years, 1961-1976.

Nelson was born of Hoosier parents in Wellington, Illinois, just across the state line from Benton County, Indiana, and he came to the Hoosier state to attend Lafayette Business College, where he studied business and accounting. Shortly after entering the business world he became, in 1927, the assistant manager of the Greater Lafayette Chamber of Commerce. George A. Nelson, "Chamber Job Got Nelson Here," Valparaiso *Vidette-Messenger,* November 4, 1976.

[8] Valparaiso *Vidette-Messenger,* November 4, 1976.

[9] The resolution by Wood is located in *Rivers and Harbors Act, U.S. Statutes at Large,* 46, Part 1 (1930): 918, 933, 942; Gary *Post-Tribune,* February 3, June 6, 1930; Pillsbury, "Subject: Burns Ditch Harbor, Indiana," March 16, 1936, IPC Files, Indiana State Archives; Gary *Post-Tribune,* December 5, 1931; Major H. J. Wild, Corps of Engineers, District Engineer, "Notice of Unfavorable Report 1930" (U.S. Engineer Office, Second Chicago District, November 8, 1930) appearing on pages 3-4 of "Northern Indiana Industrial Development Association, Appeal from adverse decision [December 21, 1935 . . . on Burns Ditch Harbor," Governor Paul V. McNutt Papers, Indiana State Archives. See John W. Larson, *Those Army Engineers: A History of the Chicago District, U.S. Army Corps of Engineers* (Chicago, 1979), 236, for a historical explanation of project application procedures relevant to the U.S. Army Corps of Engineers and Congress. Wood, a Republican legislator from Lafayette, served in Congress from 1915 until 1933, the year of his death.

[10] Frank W. Morton to Senator Sherman Minton, June 19, 1935, IPC Files, Indiana State Archives; Valparaiso *Vidette-Messenger,* November 4, 1976; "Subject: Burns Ditch Harbor Indiana, Delegation Present" [at March 16, 1936 hearing, U.S. Army Corps of Engineers, Washington, D.C.], IPC Files, Indiana State Archives.

[11] Northern Indiana Industrial Development Association (NIIDA) Statements, untitled and undated (circa 1937 and circa 1939), regarding the history of the struggle for, and the necessity of, a port on Lake Michigan, various pages, IPC Files, Indiana State Archives. NIIDA included the following organizations: Valparaiso Chamber of Commerce, Hammond Chamber of Commerce, La Porte Chamber of Commerce, Lake County Central Labor Union, Calumet Federation for the Promotion of Calumet Harbor, The Gary Boat Club, Chesterton Chamber of Commerce, Chesterton Lions Club, Porter Chamber of Commerce, and Gary Harbor Association.

[12] NIIDA Statement, [circa 1939], 5-7, IPC Files, Indiana State Archives.

[13] *Ibid.*, 8-9. See Chicago *Sunday Tribune,* August 12, 1962, and Halleck to George A. Nelson, September 10, 1937, IPC Files, Indiana State Archives. The IPC Files contain copies of some of Halleck's speeches on the floor of the House, as well as notes prepared for appearances at public hearings, regarding the Indiana port. For general information on Halleck's career, see Henry Z. Scheele, *Charlie Halleck: A Political Biography* (New York: Exposition Press, [1966]).

[14] Lt. Col. Donald H. Connolly, Corps of Engineers, U.S. War Department, U.S. Engineer Office, Chicago, "Notice of Public Hearing," August 1, 1935, IPC Files, Indiana State Archives; Lawrence M. Preston, *The Port of Indiana: Burns Waterway Harbor* (Bloomington: Bureau of Business Research, Graduate School of Business, Indiana University, [1970]), 7-9.

[15] Preston, *Port of Indiana,* 9; H. L. Gray, Midwest Steel Corporation, to Lt. Col. Donald H. Connolly, August 21, 1935; and "Resume of Report of Hearing Held on Burns Ditch Harbor Project August 22, 1935," IPC Files, Indiana State Archives.

[16] Preston, *Port of Indiana,* 7-8, Manion quotation, 8.

[17] Documents cited in text are located in IPC Files, Indiana State Archives; quotation is from S. William Sigler to P. T. [Patrick W.] Clifford, no date, *ibid.*

[18] George W. Starr to George A. Nelson, November 27, 1935, quotation on page 5; and Nelson to Starr, November 30, 1935, IPC Files, Indiana State Archives.

[19] William J. Venning to George A. Nelson, August 23, 1935; Nelson to Chicago Real Estate Board, August 24, 1935; Nelson to Venning, August 26, 1935; Venning to Nelson, July 13, 1937 with attached news clipping from Chicago *Daily News,* July 10, 1937; and Nelson memo, January 24, 1980, IPC Files, Indiana State Archives; Preston, *Port of Indiana,* 8.

[20] Nelson Oral History Interview Transcript, 10, 13, Indiana Division, Indiana State Library.

[21] Preston, *Port of Indiana,* 9; quotation from NIIDA Statement, [circa 1939], 10-11, IPC Files, Indiana State Archives.

[22] Nelson to Clarence Manion, September 11, 1935, December 27, 1935; telegram, Eugene S. Leggett to Manion, [circa September 1935]; and Sherman Minton to NIIDA, August 7, 1935, IPC Files, Indiana State Archives. See Larson, *Those Army Engineers,* 235-36, for information on the federal government's role in providing emergency work relief through river and harbor construction.

[23] Nelson Oral History Interview Transcript, 13, 31-32, Indiana Division, Indiana State Library; Preston, *Port of Indiana,* 9-10.

[24] "By Paul V. McNutt Mar 16, 1936 before U.S. Board of Army Engineers"

(seven-page typed statement with penciled label), IPC Files, Indiana State Archives.

[25] Nelson to Manion, February 22, 1936, IPC Files, Indiana State Archives; Nelson Oral History Interview Transcript, 13, Indiana Division, Indiana State Library; Pillsbury, "Subject: Burns Ditch Harbor, Indiana," March 16, 1936, IPC Files, Indiana State Archives.

[26] Nelson Oral History Interview Transcript, 13-14, Indiana Division, Indiana State Library.

[27] Preston, *Port of Indiana*, 9-11; U.S. Congress. House. Committee on Rivers and Harbors, "A Bill: Authorizing the construction, repair, and preservation of certain public works on rivers and harbors, and for other purposes," H.R. 7051, 75th Cong., 1st sess., May 24, 1937, p. 21 (printed bill); quotations from NIIDA statement, [circa 1939], 11-12; Charles A. Halleck to George A. Nelson, May 20, 1937; and S. N. Karrick, Captain, Corps of Engineers, Acting District Engineer, "Notice of Public Hearing," October 7, 1937, IPC Files, Indiana State Archives; Indianapolis *News*, July 2, 1937.

[28] "A Bill: For the improvement of Burns Ditch Harbor, Indiana," H.R. 11987, 74th Cong., 2nd sess., March 24, 1936 (typescript); George A. Nelson to Sherman Minton, December 31, 1937, IPC Files, Indiana State Archives; Gary *Post-Tribune*, January 11, 12, 1938; W. L. Phillips to Minton, January 17, 1938; and F. W. Morton to Jim Penman, secretary to Minton, January 21, 1938, IPC Files, Indiana State Archives; Valparaiso *Vidette-Messenger*, August 18, 1936; Moore, *Calumet Region*, 597-98.

[29] Nelson Oral History Interview Transcript, 10, Indiana Division, Indiana State Library; Preston, *Port of Indiana*, 13, 14, quotation, 14.

## Chapter 3, The Indiana Board of Public Harbors and Terminals

[1] George Andrew Nelson Oral History Interview Transcript, 1983, pp. 14, 35, 44-45, Oral History Project, Indiana Division, Indiana State Library; Lawrence M. Preston, *The Port of Indiana: Burns Waterway Harbor* (Bloomington: Bureau of Business Research, Graduate School of Business, Indiana University, [1970]), 11-12; Indiana *Laws*, 1939, pp. 484-86; untitled, undated paper presented by the Northern Indiana Industrial Development Association (NIIDA), Indiana Port Commission Files, Indiana State Archives.

[2] Nelson Oral History Interview Transcript, 34-35, 44, 46, Indiana Division, Indiana State Library; Thurman C. Crook to George A. Nelson, April 17, 1939; John H. Stambaugh to Harry W. Fawcett, February 24, 1939; Stambaugh to J. Frank Smith, February 24, 1939; and Stambaugh to Warren B. McAfee, February 24, 1939, IPC Files, Indiana State Archives; Indiana *Laws*, 1939, Ch. 47, p. 276. The appropriation of $50,000 was conditional, "when and if certain private corporations owning land upon and adjoining the site of the proposed harbor or channels connected therewith shall donate the necessary ground, easements and rights-of-way and shall construct one or more new industrial plants adjoining the site of the proposed harbor." *Ibid.*, 276.

[3] Indiana *Laws*, 1939, Ch. 86, pp. 484-86; Indiana Board of Public Harbors and Terminals (IBPHT), Minutes of the Organizational Meeting, June 2, 1939, Indiana State Archives. Captain Heslar (1891-1970) retired from the U.S. Navy in 1946 and was commander of the Indiana Naval Reserve. The Indianapolis Naval Armory was renamed in his honor in 1964. Indianapolis *News*, December 12, 1964, May 6, 1970.

[4] Preston, *Port of Indiana*, 13; IBPHT Minutes, July 12, November 8, 1939.

[5] IBPHT Minutes, August 4, September 12, 1939, February 22, 1940. The Mead Johnson River-Rail-Truck Terminal and Warehouse was listed in the National Register of Historic Places in 1984.

[6] *Ibid.*, March 5, 21, August 16, November 25, 1940; Senator Sherman Minton to P[atrick]. W. Clifford, President, NIIDA, January 21, 1938; George A. Nelson to Captain Samuel N. Karrick, Acting District Engineer, June 10, 1938; and Karrick to Nelson, June 11, 1938, IPC Files, Indiana State Archives.

[7] IBPHT Minutes, October 30, 1947, June 23, 1949.

[8] *Ibid.*, June 23, July 19, 1949; Preston, *Port of Indiana*, 15; U.S. Army Corps of Engineers, Chicago District, Office of the District Engineer, *Record of Public Hearing: Burns Waterway Harbor Development, Porter County, Indiana, Held at Gary, Indiana, 19 July 1949* (Chicago, 1949), 1-20 and various pages, IPC Files, Indiana State Archives. This 181-page document includes approximately forty pages of testimony and 120 pages of exhibits (statements submitted for the record) and addenda (supplementary statements submitted following the public hearing).

[9] Preston, *Port of Indiana*, 15-16; IBPHT and Indiana Economic Council, *Statement submitted for the State of Indiana at Burns Harbor, Indiana Public Hearing, Gary, Indiana, July 19, 1949*, various pages, IPC Files, Indiana State Archives.

[10] U.S. Army Corps of Engineers, *Record of Public Hearing . . . 19 July 1949*, pp. 29-33, 63-68, 110, IPC Files, Indiana State Archives.

[11] *Ibid.*, 128-37, 168-70.

[12] *Ibid.*, 52-56, 61-62, 112-19, 149-55, 171-73, 176-78, 181.

[13] Preston, *Port of Indiana*, 17-18; U.S. Army Corps of Engineers, Chicago District, *Preliminary Examination Report on Burns Waterway Harbor Development, Porter County, Indiana* (Chicago, 1950), 14, IPC Files, Indiana State Archives. This twenty-page report, plus a map of the southern lakeshore and a drawing of the "plan of improvement," was issued August 18, 1950.

[14] U.S. Department of the Army, Board of Engineers for Rivers and Harbors, *Report of Testimony and Statements Presented at the Hearing on Burns Waterway, Indiana, on 31 January 1951* (Washington, D.C., 1951), IPC Files, Indiana State Archives; Preston, *Port of Indiana*, 17-18.

[15] IBPHT, "Burns Harbor, Indiana: Statement Submitted at Public Hearing," January 31, 1951, various pages, IPC Files, Indiana State Archives; Hammond *Times*, November 28, 1950.

[16] Hammond *Times*, November 28, 1950.

[17] Preston, *Port of Indiana*, 18-19. Harland Bartholomew and Associates, *Economic Survey for the proposed Burns Harbor in Indiana* (St. Louis, 1955), 52, IPC Files, Indiana State Archives. The Harland study, in hindsight, seems to have been remarkably accurate except for the coal traffic (which failed to materialize), and the coal estimates accounted for more than ninety percent of the total of potential cargo. The modern counterpart to trailerships would be containerships, which became prevalent worldwide in the 1960s and 1970s. The use of either type of ship depended on the types of cargo shipped. J. R. Whittaker, *Containerization* (Washington, D.C.: Hemisphere Publishing Corporation, 1975), 4-13; Chicago *Tribune*, February 8, 1971.

[18] Preston, *Port of Indiana*, 19-20; Tippetts-Abbett-McCarthy-Stratton, Engineers, "Preliminary Report: Feasibility of Proposed Indiana Deepwater Port" (Draft, January 1956), two-page cover letter, and pages IV-1 to V-3, IPC Files, Indiana State Archives.

[19] Preston, *Port of Indiana*, 25.

[20] Corps of Engineers, U.S. Army Engineer District, Chicago, *Great Lakes Harbors Study, Interim Report on Burns Waterway Harbor, Indiana* (Chicago, 1960), syllabus and various pages, IPC Files, Indiana State Archives; Preston, *Port of Indiana*, 25-26.

[21] Indiana *Laws*, 1957, Ch. 286, 732-33; Preston, *Port of Indiana*, 26-29; Joseph R. Hartley, *Traffic Flow Through the Port of Indiana* (Bloomington, Ind., 1959), cover letter, and Table 1, Indiana Division, Indiana State Library. Preston, a research associate of Professor Hartley at the time, considered this report "a landmark in the history of Burns Harbor planning and development" (*Port of Indiana*, 28).

[22] Preston, *Port of Indiana*, 28-29; Gary *Post-Tribune*, July 2, 1959; Indianapolis *News*, July 2, 1959.

## Chapter 4, Establishing the Indiana Port Commission

[1] Kay Franklin and Norma Schaeffer, *Duel for the Dunes: Land Use Conflict on the Shores of Lake Michigan* (Urbana: University of Illinois Press, 1983), 127, 149. The statement quoted was made by George Applegate, executive secretary of the East Chicago Chamber of Commerce, during an interview with Franklin and Schaeffer in 1977. Despite its virtues, this book's overall value is somewhat compromised by biases and errors, particularly regarding the motivations of port proponents.

[2] *Congressional Record*, 85th Cong., 2nd sess. (1958), 104, pt. 7:9468-72. Also see Paul H. Douglas, *In the Fullness of Time: The Memoirs of Paul H. Douglas* (New York: Harcourt Brace Jovanovich, Inc., 1971).

[3] Franklin and Schaeffer, *Duel for the Dunes*, 137-38; Douglas, *In the Fullness of Time*, 537. Also see statewide newspaper coverage of these events; some clippings are in the Indiana Port Commission Files, Indiana State Archives.

[4] Corps of Engineers, U.S. Army Engineer District, Chicago, *Great Lakes Harbors Study, Interim Report on Burns Waterway Harbor, Indiana* (Chicago, 1960), IPC Files, Indiana State Archives; Lawrence M. Preston, *The Port of Indiana: Burns Waterway Harbor* (Bloomington: Bureau of Business Research, Graduate School of Business, Indiana University, [1970]), 31.

[5] Preston, *Port of Indiana*, 14, 33-34; Indiana *Laws*, 1959, Ch. 343, Sec. 21; *ibid.*, 1961, Ch. 11, Sec. 2b.

[6] Matthew E. Welsh, *View from the State House: Recollections and Reflections, 1961-1965* (Indianapolis: Indiana Historical Bureau, 1981), 11, 68.

[7] Indiana *Laws*, 1961, Ch. 11. See Appendix for complete list of commissioners.

[8] *Ibid.*, 1957, Ch. 286, Sec. 6, 1961, Ch. 11.

[9] IPC Agenda and Minutes, April 10, 1961; interview with Robert M. Schram and William H. Keck, June 23, 1990, Mount Vernon, Indiana; Chicago *Daily News*, April 10, 1961, Red Streak edition.

[10] IPC Minutes, April 10, 1961, p. 5. These minutes indicate that the sec-

ond Port Commission meeting was scheduled for May 4, 1961; it was actually held on May 3. Hurt was an experienced politician who had been Governor Paul V. McNutt's law partner. He also had been one of Governor Welsh's law school classmates and one of his chief political strategists during the 1960 campaign. Welsh, *View from the State House,* 11-12.

[11] IPC Minutes, May 3, 1961; "Notice of Public Hearing" and list of persons testifying, *ibid.* Recordings were made of the entire proceedings on five seven-inch reel-to-reel tapes; the author made extensive notes on the contents of the tapes. The narrative about the public hearing on May 3, 1961 is based on the notes from those tape recordings of the proceedings.

[12] IPC Minutes, May 18, 1961. The "Report to the Indiana Port Commission," by the Land and Physical Development Committee appointed on May 3, is included with these minutes.

[13] Edward H. Frank, "About the Port," Indianapolis *Star,* April 15, 1962, includes diagrams of the land proposals in the bills.

[14] John I. Bradshaw, Jr. to James R. Fleming, July 6, 1961, Governor Welsh Papers, Indiana State Archives; *Orbison* v. *Welsh, Governor of Indiana et al.* (1961), 242 Indiana 385. An important precedent-setting case for this decision was *Ennis* v. *State Highway Commission of Indiana et al.* (1952), 231 Indiana 311.

[15] Franklin and Schaeffer, *Duel for the Dunes,* 140, 145.

[16] Matthew E. Welsh, "To the Friends of Indiana," August 14, 1961, IPC Files, Indiana State Archives; four-page memorandum attached to Clinton Green to Governor Welsh, August 14, 1961, Governor Welsh Papers, Indiana State Archives; Indianapolis *Star,* August 30, 1961.

[17] Indianapolis *Star,* August 31, 1961. Congressman J. Edward Roush of Huntington sponsored the House bill.

[18] Indianapolis *Star,* August 31, 1961.

[19] Handley, "Why The Port Of Indiana Is A Necessity," *Indiana Business and Industry* (September 1961), 16-18. Handley's arguments reinforced a report regarding the difficulties of ships entering the older facilities at Calumet Harbor. There, ships had to pass what captains called "the 'iron curtain'"—the fourteen bridges across the Calumet River that had to be opened to permit ships to pass. The average time required to navigate the six and one-half-mile channel was two and a half hours, although at times it required up to six hours. Ships also required a special river pilot and one or two tugboats. "When series of ships go up the river," according to the Chicago *Tribune,* "they look like rhumba lines in slow motion as the ships negotiate more than 10 sharp bends in the river's course." The *Tribune* also commented on Chicago's difficulties in floating general revenue bonds to improve the port at Lake Calumet because of the anticipated "competition from Indiana's proposed seaports at Burns Ditch and Indiana Harbor." Chicago *Tribune,* December 27, 1959.

[20] Handley, "Why The Port Of Indiana Is A Necessity."

[21] Preston, *Port of Indiana,* 37-38.

## Chapter 5, Funding and Construction on Lake Michigan
[1] New York *Times,* March 11, 1962.

[2] Indianapolis *News,* July 5, 1962; New York *Times,* July 6, 1962.

[3] Fort Wayne *News-Sentinel,* October 4, 1962; Indianapolis *News,* October 4, 1962.

[4] Charles McCuen, substituting for O'Connor on October 11, 1962, focused on a purchase of dunes sand by Northwestern University, Evanston, Illinois. James W. Chester, a Valparaiso attorney and son of the man who had broached the idea of a Burns Harbor port to George Nelson, responded with praise for McCuen and condemnation of O'Connor. James W. Chester to Charles McCuen, Chicago, October 13, 1962, Indiana Port Commission Files, Indiana State Archives. The letter was prompted by McCuen's "accurate" report concerning Northwestern University. Chester also attempted to correct misstatements by Senator Douglas and other conservationists in his five-page letter. See also Paul H. Douglas, *In the Fullness of Time: The Memoirs of Paul H. Douglas* (New York: Harcourt Brace Jovanovich, Inc., 1972), 538.

[5] Lee C. White to Governor Matthew E. Welsh, October 29, 1962, IPC Files, Indiana State Archives.

[6] IPC Minutes, May 16, 1962. The initial legislation authorizing the Port Commission (Indiana *Laws,* 1961, Ch. 11) mandated that the state attorney general's office provide legal counsel to the commission. Over the years, the legal services of the attorney general's office have been extensive and significant in handling land acquisitions, lease arrangements, various issues in litigation, and other matters.

[7] Indiana *House Journal,* 1963, pp. 23, 24.

[8] Matthew E. Welsh, *View from the State House: Recollections and Reflections, 1961-1965* (Indianapolis: Indiana Historical Bureau, 1981), 150, 177-78.

[9] Indiana *Laws,* 1963 special session, 149; *ibid.,* regular session, 1096. See Welsh, *View from the State House,* 178-82, for his review of the negotiations for economic development.

[10] IPC Minutes, July 3, 11, 1963 (the signed agreement is included with the July 11 minutes). According to Commissioner Schram, the firm's senior partner Lief J. Sverdrup personally responded to the Port Commission's overture in June, stopping in Indianapolis en route home from New York City. Sverdrup was a commanding general in the Corps of Engineers in World War II. Obituary, New York *Times,* January 3, 1976.

[11] Sverdrup & Parcel and Associates, Inc., *Burns Waterway Harbor Interim Report* (St. Louis, 1964), *passim;* Indianapolis *Star,* January 12, 1964. Unless otherwise indicated, the discussion that follows in the text and in this note is based on these sources.

The key consultants in preparing the Sverdrup & Parcel report were James C. Buckley, Inc., of New York City, who took primary responsibility for the economic feasibility studies; and Arthur G. Keller, Inc. and E. Lee Heidenreich, Jr., who laid out the specifications for a sugar refinery and the grain elevators. The Coastal Engineering Laboratory at the University of Florida did the model studies of Lake Michigan, analyzing wind and water activities according to different port design configurations. Merrill, Lynch, Pierce, Fenner and Smith, Inc. served as the project's financial consultants.

The major limitation of the report seems to have been some overly ambitious planning of port facilities that had to be scaled back when construction began. There were also some errors in the historical summary of the project, which perpetuated the incorrect Daniel Webster connection. In all respects, however, it admirably suited the promotional purposes of the Port Commission as it prepared to carry an appeal for port construction funding to the Indiana General Assembly. The selection of Sverdrup & Parcel proved to be a wise choice; there was a long, harmonious, and mutually advantageous relationship that covered the construction of Indiana's three public ports.

[12] "The State of Indiana 1990," *Area Development* (1990), 35.

[13] Indiana *House Journal*, 1965, pp. 19-20. Clinton Green had caused some momentary concern when he decided to seek the Democratic nomination for governor in 1964. The commission has prided itself on its minimal partisanship; Green's political plans meant he had to resign from the commission, which he did early in 1964. The enabling legislation specified that "The commission shall consist of five (5) members . . . no more than three (3) of whom shall be members of the same political party." Indiana *Laws*, 1961, Ch. 11, Sec. 3. Naturally, the balance generally was in favor of the governor's party. See Appendix for complete list of commissioners.

[14] Indiana *House Journal*, 1965, p. 47.

[15] Indiana *Laws*, 1965, pp. 441, 528-30.

[16] *Ibid.*, 608; a 1934 federal statute, cited in this law, authorized establishment of foreign trade zones.

[17] Indianapolis *Star*, July 22, 1965.

[18] *Ibid.*

[19] *U.S. Statutes at Large* 79 (1965): 1091. It is significant that rather than *approval* of a park, the legislation called only for a *vote* on the park; if the park was not authorized, the port could still go forward.

[20] IPC *Annual Report*, 1966, has a convenient summary of events and actions in 1965-1966; Sverdrup & Parcel and Associates, Inc., "Burns Waterway Harbor Design Memorandum," December 1965, IPC Files, Indiana State Archives. See also IPC Minutes, October 25, 1965, June 2, 21, 1966.

[21] Chesterton *Tribune*, October 10, 1966. The IPC Files, Indiana State Archives, contain a tape recording of the day's festivities, taken from a Valparaiso radio station's live broadcast.

[22] Chesterton *Tribune*, October 10, 1966. See Douglas, *In the Fullness of Time*, 542-43, regarding final passage of the park bill; it became Public Law 89-761, *U.S. Statutes at Large* 80 (1966): 1309.

[23] The bottom layer consisted of 570,094 cubic yards of sand backfill and sand core. The second layer consisted of 555,700 tons of core stone, weighing five to ninety pounds each, shipped from Rogers City, Michigan. The third layer of "W-10" stone, in blocks weighing from 1,500 to 3,000 pounds each, had come by barge from Joliet, Illinois. The top three layers consisted of Indiana limestone, brought by rail from Bedford, Indiana, amounting to 470,540 tons of blocks weighing three to twenty tons each. A total of 1,248,140 tons of stone was used for the north breakwater. This information is taken from an undated one-page document, "Cross Section of Breakwater," and a one-page sketch dated February 1 and 4, 1966, IPC Files, Indiana State Archives.

[24] "New Deep Water Harbor for Indiana," *Kie-Ways* (November/December 1968), 10-12, IPC Files, Indiana State Archives; interview with Robert M. Schram and William H. Keck, June 23, 1990, Mount Vernon, Indiana.

[25] IPC *Annual Report*, 1969. Information that follows in the text is based

on this source unless otherwise indicated.

²⁶ Fitzgerald served well during his decade and more as port director, overseeing the completion and first years of operation at Burns Harbor and the construction of a second port on the Ohio River at Mount Vernon.

²⁷ Indiana *Laws,* 1969, p. 1715.

## Chapter 6, Getting Started: The First Decade of Operations

¹ Interview with Robert M. Schram and William H. Keck, June 23, 1990, Mount Vernon, Indiana. The Indianapolis *Star* carried a major story regarding plans for the two-day affair in its Sunday, July 5, 1970 issue; U.S. Secretary of Transportation John A. Volpe was scheduled as the principal speaker. Although admittedly dedicating what new Indiana Port Commission chairman Joseph N. Thomas called a "bare bones" port, the port had already received its first foreign vessel. The Yugoslavian freighter, SS *Banja Luka,* had picked up a cargo of scrap steel for shipment to Japan. Gary *Post-Tribune,* July 1, 1970. See also Indiana Port Commission Files, Indiana State Archives, for information regarding the dedication festivities and ceremonies. U.S. Senator Birch E. Bayh and former Congressman Charles A. Halleck were among the featured speakers. The publication included in the press kit was *The Port of Indiana: Burns Waterway Harbor,* by Lawrence M. Preston (Bloomington: Bureau of Business Research, Graduate School of Business, Indiana University, [1970]); IPC Files, *ibid.*

² IPC *Annual Report,* 1970, Introduction; Gary *Post-Tribune,* July 16, 1970. The 1970 *Annual Report* also notes that the commission closed its Indianapolis office in mid-1970 and "all administrative activities were consolidated in the new administrative building at the [Burns Harbor] Port site" p. [2].

³ IPC *Annual Report,* 1976, pp. 1, 6-7, 1977, pp. 1, 7.

⁴ See IPC *Annual Report,* 1976, 1977, 1978, 1979. See especially the statement by Ray Sierra, business agent of the International Longshoreman's Association, one of a number of "testimonials" to the efficacy of the port. *Ibid.,* 1977, p. 5.

⁵ IPC *Annual Report,* 1983, pp. 2-4.

⁶ *Ibid.,* 1979, pp. [1, 3], 1981. The 1981 report contains a brief account, on pages 5 and 6, of dedication ceremonies at Cargill's elevator in August. That same month, the *Canadoc,* a 600-foot Great Lakes freighter, was the first vessel to load grain at the facility.

⁷ IPC *Annual Report,* 1979, p. [3], 1981, pp. 5, 6; IPC, *Tide-ings,* July 1973, p. [2]; Cass Vincent to Jack Fitzgerald, October 10, 1975, IPC Files, Indiana State Archives; "Remarks by Jack P. Fitzgerald, Port Director, Port of Indiana," American Association of Port Authorities 62nd Convention, *Proceedings and Papers* (1974), 61-64; IPC, *Tide-ings,* January 1973, p. [1].

⁸ IPC *Annual Report,* 1975, 1980, introductory and financial statements. More barges than ships called at the port since they had year-round access, but barges carried less total cargo.

⁹ Northwest Ordinance, 1787, art. 4; U.S. Constitution, art. 1, sec. 10; Rivers and Harbors Appropriation Act of 1884, in *Laws of the United States relating to the Improvement of Rivers and Harbors from August 11, 1790 to June 29, 1938* (3 vols., Washington, D.C.: U.S. Government Printing Office,

1940), 1:415; "Memorandum," Robert D. Kraft, executive director, to members, Indiana Port Commission, December 29, 1987, IPC Files, Indiana State Archives.

[10] IPC Minutes, July 29, 1976; *Indiana Port Commission* v. *Bethlehem Steel Corporation and Lake Carriers' Association,* U.S. Court of Appeals, No. 87-1290 (7th Circuit, 1987); Matthew E. Welsh, *View from the State House: Recollections and Reflections, 1961-1965* (Indianapolis: Indiana Historical Bureau, 1981), 68. The court decision reviews the history of the litigation since 1971; the case was argued October 26 and decided December 23, 1987.

[11] Interview with Schram and Keck; George Andrew Nelson Oral History Interview Transcript, 1983, pp. 23, 46, Oral History Project, Indiana Division, Indiana State Library.

[12] Nelson Oral History Interview Transcript, 23; *Indiana Port Commission* v. *Bethlehem Steel Corporation and Lake Carriers' Association;* IPC Minutes, March 15, 1974, February 24, 1988.

[13] Sverdrup & Parcel and Associates, Inc., *Burns Waterway Harbor Interim Report* (St. Louis, 1964), 35, Indiana Division, Indiana State Library.

[14] *Ibid.,* 51; IPC *Annual Report,* 1969, 1971, 1972, 1973, financial statements.

[15] IPC Minutes, September 5, 1975; Indiana *Laws,* 1965, pp. 441-43; *ibid.,* 1971, pp. 420-23; IPC *Annual Report,* 1970, 1972, 1973, 1974, 1975, *passim.* For example, in 1980 the revenue at Burns Harbor consisted of $973,000 in rental income, $286,000 in wharfage, $69,000 in dockage, $26,000 from the sale of sand, $12,000 in harbor service fees (before being disallowed by the courts), and $15,000 in miscellaneous income, for a total of $1,381,000. This provided an income in excess of operating expenses of more than $400,000 before depreciation, which resulted in a net deficit of $460,000. Investment income for the year, however, exceeded $2,700,000, leaving a net income for the year of $2,211,000. *Ibid.,* 1980, pp. [9-12].

[16] IPC *Annual Report,* 1973, p. [1], 1974, pp. 6, 8; Jacques LesStrang, *The Great Lakes St. Lawrence System* (Harbor Island, Maple City, Mich.: Harbor House Publishers, Inc., 1984), 4-5, 10; Bill Beck to Indiana Historical Bureau, January 20, 1996, Indiana Historical Bureau Port History Files, Indiana State Archives; Carleton Mabee, *The Seaway Story* (New York: The Macmillan Company, 1961), 61, 67, 114, 167-68, 262-65. LesStrang's book is a brief, readable, and well-illustrated history of the St. Lawrence Seaway. Bill Beck served as a commissioner of the Seaway Port Authority of Duluth, Minnesota, from 1982 to 1988.

According to Beck, "The 'thousand-footers,' as they were known in the Great Lakes maritime community, revolutionized the movement of bulk cargo on the Great Lakes. Primarily used to haul taconite and low-sulfur coal downbound from Lake Superior to the lower lakes, the thousand-footers were bigger, faster and more efficient than the 500- [to] 800-foot ore boats that made up the bulk of the Great Lakes fleet in the 1950s and 1960s. Outfitted with self-unloading deck equipment and bow thrusters for maneuverability in tight channels, the thousand-footer can move 60,000 tons of taconite pellets from Duluth-Superior to lower Lake Michigan steel mills in three days, off-load the cargo in six to twelve hours and be upbound to Lake Superior ports for another load of taconite pellets in an additional three days' time. As a consequence of the commissioning of a dozen thousand-footers between 1970 and 1979, the industry began to retire older ore boats and consolidate its fleet . . . . Today, the Great Lakes fleet of 65 boats moves approximately 60 million tons of taconite pellets, coal and limestone during the annual navigation season.

"Because of their size, the thousand-footers were unable to transit the Welland Locks bypassing Niagara Falls and were constrained to operating only in Lakes Superior, Michigan, Huron and Erie." Bill Beck to Indiana Historical Bureau, June 24, 1996. IHB Port History Files, Indiana State Archives.

[17] IPC *Annual Report,* 1973, pp. [5-6], 1974, p. 5, 1975, p. 7; David G. Abraham to Ralph D. Gray, August 15, 1990 with attached "Synopsis of Representative Projects . . . ," IHB Port History Files, Indiana State Archives.

[18] IPC, *Tide-ings,* January 1973, p. 1; IPC *Annual Report,* 1973, p. [1]; IPC Minutes, March 30, 1973, December 15, 1972.

[19] IPC *Annual Report,* 1973, p. [1], 1974, p. 8, and related materials. See also William J. Watt, *Bowen: The Years as Governor* (Indianapolis: Bierce Associates Inc., 1981), 115, 223.

[20] IPC *Annual Report,* 1980, *passim;* Indianapolis *News,* March 23, 1978, December 13, 1979; Indianapolis *Star,* February 22, 23, 1980; Indiana *Laws,* 1961, p. 16.

[21] Interview with Schram and Keck.

[22] *Ibid.;* Indiana *Laws,* 1975, p. 593. See Appendix for a complete list of commissioners.

[23] IPC *Annual Report,* 1974, p. 9; interview with Schram and Keck. Abraham provided the expertise (and the stimulus) for dozens of motor carriers to obtain the requisite operating authorities from the Interstate Commerce Commission and the Indiana Public Service Commission, thereby providing motor carrier service to the Indiana ports, and to get Burns Harbor included within the Chicago Commercial Zone (over the opposition of some sixty Chicago-based trucking companies). He also developed and filed with the Federal Maritime Commission various tariff schedules for the Port Commission, offered expert testimony before state and federal legislative committees and in various judicial proceedings, and represented the Port Commission before port authorities, trade associations, and the rate-making and tariff-publishing bureaus of the railroad and barge industries. Abraham to Gray, August 15, 1990 with attached "Synopsis of Representative Projects . . . ," IHB Port History Files, Indiana State Archives.

[24] IPC Minutes, June 28, September 10, 1976. Following Nelson's death in 1985, the main road leading into Burns Harbor was named Nelson Drive in his honor. *Ibid.,* October 23, 1985.

### Chapter 7, Accessing the Ohio River: Southwind Maritime Centre

[1] Indiana Board of Public Harbors and Terminals, Meeting Minutes, February 22, 1940, p. 113; Governor Matthew E. Welsh, three-page statement, January 4, 1963, Indiana Port Commission Files, Indiana State Archives; Matthew E. Welsh, *View from the State House: Recollections and Reflections, 1961-1965* (Indianapolis: Indiana Historical Bureau, 1981), 173-82; Indiana *Laws,* 1963, pp. 1096-99 and special session, 149.

Dillin also intended to repeal the 1947 resolution against federal aid for Indiana. Repeal was accomplished without fanfare, one of the conditions insisted upon by Republicans who had supported the resolution originally.

"So far as I know," Dillin wrote in Welsh's 1981 book, "no newspaper ever ran a story on this occurrence, and I really doubt that any of them ever found out what was going on." Welsh, *View from the State House,* 76-77, 238-41, quotation is on page 241. See also Charles Francis Fleming, *The White Hat: Henry F. Schricker, A Political Biography* ([Indianapolis], 1966), 108-15, regarding the federal aid resolution of 1947.

² *Big Load Afloat: U.S. Domestic Water Transportation Resources* (Washington, D.C.: American Waterways Operators, Inc., 1973), 8-10; *Preliminary Report of the Inland Waterways Commission, Senate Documents,* 17, pp. i-vii, 1-27; *U.S. Statutes at Large* 37 (1912): 566; *ibid.,* 41 (1920): 499; quotation is *ibid.,* 43 (1924): 360.

³ Sverdrup & Parcel and Associates, Inc., *Southwest Indiana Ohio River Port Feasibility Report* (St. Louis, 1970), i-20, IPC Files, Indiana State Archives. This study contains a short history of Ohio River improvements made during the nineteenth and early twentieth centuries.

⁴ *Big Load Afloat,* 1-52; interview with Southwind Maritime Centre Port Director Donald R. Snyder, Mount Vernon, Indiana, March 16, 1990.

⁵ *Big Load Afloat,* 10-18, 23-33. At the Port of Chicago, for example, plagued by a series of low bridges, special towboats equipped with telescoping pilothouses were developed in order to get the boats under the bridges. *Ibid.,* 18.

⁶ Sverdrup & Parcel and Associates, Inc., *Feasibility Report,* 1970, p. 4.

⁷ Interview with Robert M. Schram and William H. Keck, Mount Vernon, Indiana, June 23, 1990; Indianapolis *Star,* July 18, 1971; Indiana *Laws,* 1963, p. 1096, and 1969, pp. 1596, 1715. The Mead Johnson River-Rail-Truck Terminal and Warehouse was listed in the National Register of Historic Places in 1984.

⁸ Sverdrup & Parcel and Associates, Inc., *Feasibility Report,* 1970, *passim.* A towhead is a low alluvial island or shoal in a river.

⁹ *Ibid.*

¹⁰ Keck operated one of the oldest (since 1912) continuous Ford dealerships in the state of Indiana, an automobile sales business that had been started by his father in 1907. *Keck, Indiana's Oldest Ford Dealer,* pamphlet (Mount Vernon, Ind., n.d.), Indiana Historical Bureau Port History Files, Indiana State Archives. A Democrat, Keck succeeded Henry R. Sackett of Gary as a member of the Port Commission. Despite his remoteness from the Port Commission headquarters, which had been moved to Burns Harbor in 1970, Keck kept his travel time to a minimum often by flying his own plane to commission meetings. Interview with Schram and Keck. See Appendix for a complete list of commissioners.

¹¹ J. R. Whittaker, *Containerization* (Washington, D.C.: Hemisphere Publishing Corporation, 1975), 4-21; *Big Load Afloat,* 44, 46, 107-11; Indianapolis *Star,* November 12, 1985; quotation is from Mount Vernon *Democrat,* June 1, 1973.

¹² Indiana *Laws,* 1971, pp. 2223, 2225; interview with Schram and Keck. The authority to condemn land by legal process had to be used against one holdout landowner, but he agreed to an out-of-court settlement after the condemnation suit had been instituted. IPC Minutes, November 3, 1972, p. 212,

December 15, 1972, p. 227, January 26, 1973, p. 258.

[13] IPC *Annual Report,* 1973, p. [9]; Indiana *Laws,* 1973, pp. 1964-65; IPC Minutes, February 23, 1973.

[14] The assessment was reported in Thomas J. Green, *An Archaeological Survey of the Wabash River Valley in Posey and Gibson Counties, Indiana* (Bloomington: Glenn A. Black Laboratory of Archaeology, Indiana University, 1972). In 1978, a Mississippian village site was discovered on the port property. In 1980, 600 acres—most of the port property—was surveyed. In 1981-1982, several stages of excavation were carried out at the Mississippian village site to assess its significance and then to mitigate the impact of industrial development. The 1980s excavation revealed a significant six-acre village site—a walled, rectangular complex surrounding numerous houses and a central plaza. Before it was destroyed by construction, forty percent of the Southwind site was examined—compared to two percent of the Mississippian town site preserved as Angel Mounds State Historic Site. Cheryl Ann Munson to Indiana Historical Bureau, July 29, 1996; Sharon Sorenson, "Southwind Dig," *Outdoor Indiana* (June 1983), 25-29; James H. Kellar, *An Archaeological Reconnaissance of a Portion of the Southwind Maritime Centre, Posey County, Indiana* (Bloomington: Glenn A. Black Laboratory of Archaeology, Indiana University, 1980); Ruth A. Brinker and Cheryl Ann Munson, *An Archaeological Reconnaissance of the Southwind Maritime Centre, Posey County, Indiana* (Bloomington: Glenn A. Black Laboratory of Archaeology, Indiana University, 1981); Cheryl Ann Munson, ed., *Archaeological Investigations at the Southwind Site, A Mississippian Community in Posey County, Indiana* (review draft prepared for Indiana Port Commission, March 1994).

[15] Mount Vernon *Democrat,* June 2, 1973. Deckard's efforts in the 1967 session to get legislative authorization for a Mount Vernon port had failed, but he returned in 1969 "with greater determination and knowledge" as well as powerful allies, particularly then Senator Orr and Senator Will Ulrich of Aurora. *Ibid.,* June 1, 1973; Indiana *Laws,* 1969, pp. 1596, 1714-15; interview with Schram and Keck. Orr served as state senator, 1969, 1971-1972, as lieutenant governor, 1973-1981, and as governor, 1981-1989.

[16] Mount Vernon *Democrat,* June 1, 1973; *ibid.,* June 2, 1973 provides additional coverage of the groundbreaking.

[17] IPC *Annual Report,* 1976, pp. 1, 10, 11; Indiana Port Commission, *Southwind Maritime Centre* (brochure, Indianapolis, n.d.), [3]; Indiana Port Commission, *Industrial Development Guide, Southwind Maritime Centre* (Indianapolis, 1986), [3, 4]; IPC Minutes, May 25, 1977.

[18] IPC *Annual Report,* 1976, p. 10, 1977, p. 7, 1980, pp. [5, 6], 1981, pp. 6, 7, 1982, pp. 1-4, 1983, pp. 3-4. The local name for the MAPCO facility was the Mount Vernon Coal Transfer Company.

[19] IPC *Annual Report,* 1978, p. [1]; IPC Minutes, May 31, 1984, p. 2; IPC *Annual Report,* 1984, p. [13]. Allen, according to the minutes, "offered quick action in assignments relating to acquiring goods and services for the Port Commission; his day-to-day management skills maintained high morale at Southwind and Clark Maritime Centres; and his eagerness to pursue marketing assignments and special knowledge of transportation is difficult to duplicate." At the time of his death, Allen was president of the Inland Rivers, Ports, and Terminals Association.

[20] Kinnett came to the Port Commission after working in trucking and marine operations. In 1989, he relinquished his responsibilities at Southwind to Donald R. Snyder. IPC Minutes, August 28, 1984; IPC *Annual Report, 1984,* p. 7; IPC, *Portside,* Summer 1989, p. [2].

[21] IPC *Annual Report,* 1984, pp. 1, 2, 4, 5; Indianapolis *Star,* March 20, 1991; IPC Minutes, January 30, 1976; Indiana *Laws,* 1976, pp. 131-32; Michael Przybylski and Drew Klacik, *The Ports of the Indiana Port Commission: Economic Impacts and Economic Development* (Indianapolis: Center for Urban Policy and the Environment, School of Public and Environmental Affairs, Indiana University, July 1994), 26. A dolphin is a structure to which a vessel may be moored in open water.

[22] IPC Minutes, January 30, 1976, October 27, 1982.

## Chapter 8, A Second Ohio River Port: Clark Maritime Centre

[1] Indiana Port Commission, *Tide-ings,* July 1973, p. [1]; Indiana *Laws,* 1971, p. 2225; Sverdrup & Parcel and Associates, Inc., *Southeast Indiana Ohio River Port Feasibility Report* (St. Louis, 1972), i, iii, 1, 19-22, Indiana Division, Indiana State Library.

[2] Sverdrup & Parcel and Associates, Inc., *Southeast Indiana Ohio River Port Feasibility Report,* iii, 37-38, 50, 94-95. Another significant factor in the selection decision was that river fluctuations between high and normal levels were 42.4 feet at Jeffersonville, but 75.4 feet at New Albany, located downriver from the Falls of the Ohio at Louisville. *Ibid.,* 95.

[3] *Ibid.,* iii-iv, 56-65, 100-1, and introductory letter, L. J. Sverdrup to Indiana Port Commission, June 29, 1972.

[4] *Ibid.,* 99.

[5] Indiana *Laws,* 1973, p. 1965; Louisville *Times,* December 7, 1972; IPC, *Tide-ings,* July 1973, p. [1] reports on Governor Bowen's comments.

[6] IPC Minutes, May 31, August 30, 1974; Governor Bowen statement, September 10, 1974, Indiana Port Commission Files, Indiana State Archives.

[7] IPC *Annual Report,* 1976, pp. 12-13; IPC Minutes, August 30, 1974, January 30, February 27, 1976, February 4, April 15, 1977.

[8] Lieutenant Governor Robert D. Orr to Governor Otis R. Bowen, October 3, 1975; Orr to Cyrus MacKinnon (Executive Vice President, The Louisville *Courier Journal & Times*), October 3, 1975; and James H. Kellar to Honorable Richard Wathen, House of Representatives, Indianapolis, January 21, 1976, IPC Files, Indiana State Archives; Indianapolis *Star,* November 28, 1979.

[9] Louisville *Courier-Journal,* March 10, 1976.

[10] *Ibid.*

[11] *Ibid.;* U.S. Army Corps of Engineers, Louisville District, Kentucky, *Draft Environmental Impact Statement: Clark Maritime Centre,* October 1975, pp. a-1 to a-5, Indiana Division, Indiana State Library. This was also the position of the Admirals Anchor Marina, Inc. (4000 Utica Pike, Jeffersonville, Indiana), which used the channel between the north bank of the Ohio River and Sixmile Island for entering its own harbor. According to the marina's secretary-treasurer, hundreds of pleasure craft used it regularly, an expansion was being planned, and the marina believed the channel could not serve both ports. The marina, therefore, requested that the Port Commission withdraw its applica-

tion for a construction permit and threatened a lawsuit if one was issued. William R. Vissing to the Indiana Port Commission, April 16, 1976, IPC Files, Indiana State Archives.

[12] IPC Minutes, January 30, 1976; Kellar to Wathen, January 21, 1976, with attached correspondence and nomination to the National Register of Historic Places, IPC Files, Indiana State Archives; IPC *Annual Report,* 1976, p. 12. Kellar had forwarded a copy of his Clark Maritime Centre report to Wathen, along with the explanatory cover letter, a copy of which he also sent to the Port Commission's engineer, C. Thomas Bagley. The site was not placed in the National Register of Historic Places, but it is listed in the Indiana Register of Historic Sites and Structures.

[13] Kellar to Wathen, January 21, 1976, IPC Files, Indiana State Archives.

[14] IPC Minutes, January 30, 1976; "Memorandum for Record," February 5, 1976, prepared by James B. Meanor, Sverdrup & Parcel, and C. Thomas Bagley, IPC Files, Indiana State Archives. Pfau was one of two new commissioners appointed when the Port Commission was enlarged from five to seven members because of expanded responsibilities, literally from one end of the state to the other. The second new commissioner appointed at this time was William E. Babincsak, a former member of the Indiana General Assembly from Lake County. IPC Minutes, 1976, 1977. See the Appendix for a complete list of commissioners.

[15] "Memorandum for Record," February 5, 1976, IPC Files, Indiana State Archives. The "State historic preservation Screening Board," first known as the Indiana Professional State Consulting Committee to the National Register of Historic Places, is now known as the Indiana Historic Preservation Review Board. See Indiana Code 14-21-1-20-22 for details on this board.

[16] IPC *Annual Report,* 1976, pp. 12-13; IPC Minutes, January 30, February 27, April 9, 1976. The mitigation was handled by a private archaeological service, Resource Analysts, Inc., of Bloomington, Indiana.

[17] Louisville District Corps of Engineers, Notice of Public Hearing, April 8, 1976, IPC Files, Indiana State Archives; IPC Agenda Notes, May 26, 1976, p. [2], and Minutes, May 26, 1976; IPC *Annual Report,* 1977, p. 7, 1978, p. 1.

[18] *Kentucky* v. *Indiana,* 440 U.S. 902 (1979); IPC Minutes, July 20, 1979; Indianapolis *News,* November 10, 1978.

[19] IPC Minutes, March 10, September 23, 1982; Indianapolis *News,* November 10, 1978, July 22, 1981; *Kentucky ex rel. Beshear* v. *Alexander,* 655 *Federal Reporter* 2d 714 (6th Cir. 1981). For information on the case of *Kentucky* v. *Indiana,* see the various orders of the Supreme Court recorded at 440 U.S. 902 (1979), when the case was filed; 441 U.S. 941 (1979), appointing a Special Master; 444 U.S. 816 (1979), noting receipt in October 1979 of the Special Master's report; and, following additional motions, 456 U.S. 958 (1982), noting receipt and filing of the final report in May 1982. A similar case, *Ohio* v. *Kentucky,* filed in December 1979 and decided on January 21, 1980, had elicited a lengthy decision by the Supreme Court, 444 U.S. 335 (1980), which established Kentucky's boundary as it existed in 1792, when Kentucky was admitted to the Union and not at the current low-water mark. The Ohio case was controlled by *Indiana* v. *Kentucky,* 136 U.S. 479 (1890), involving land on the Indiana side of the Ohio River in Evansville that, according to the court, belonged to Kentucky, since the river had changed course between

1792 and 1889.

[20] IPC *Annual Report,* 1982, pp. 1, 4-5, 8; Indianapolis *News,* June 2, 1982; Indianapolis *Star,* April 7, 1983; IPC *Annual Report,* 1984, pp. 8, 9, 1985, p. 2.

[21] Indianapolis *News,* June 16, 1987; IPC *Annual Report,* 1984, p. 1, 1985, p. 2; Merchants Grain, Inc., *Merchants Grain is Bulk Handling, Storage, Direct Transfer . . .* (brochure, n.p., n.d.), IHB Port History Files, Indiana State Archives; Indianapolis *Star,* November 12, 1985; Indiana Port Commission, *Clark Maritime Centre: Industrial Development Guide* (brochure, circa 1990), IHB Port History Files, Indiana State Archives.

[22] Indianapolis *Star,* April 16, 1988; "Clark Maritime Centre Comparative Tonnage—1988/1989," IHB Port History Files, Indiana State Archives; Indiana Port Commission, *Clark Maritime Centre: Industrial Development Guide, ibid.;* IPC, *Indiana Portside,* Summer 1994, 9; quotation is in IPC *Annual Report,* 1984, p. 1.

### Chapter 9, Moving to the Future

[1] Indianapolis *News,* June 16, 1987.

[2] IPC Minutes, May 31, 1984, p. 5; IPC *Annual Report,* 1984, p. 1; interview with Robert M. Schram and William H. Keck, June 23, 1990, Mount Vernon, Indiana.

[3] IPC *Annual Report,* 1984, p. 6; Indiana Port Commission Report of 1984 Significa to Governor Robert D. Orr by IPC Chairman Quentin A. Blachly, 3, 4.

[4] IPC Minutes, August 27, 1984, p. 7; IPC *Annual Report,* 1984, p. 5.

[5] Indiana Port Commission Strategic Marketing Plan, 1996 to 2000, February 26, 1996, pp. 18-19, Indiana Historical Bureau Port History Files, Indiana State Archives.

[6] IPC *Annual Report,* 1981, pp. 1, 5, 1985, p. [4].

[7] IPC *Annual Report,* 1975, p. 6; IPC, *Indiana Portside,* Spring 1994, p. 5; Indianapolis *Star,* October 5, 1989.

[8] IPC *Annual Report,* 1980, pp. [5, 6], 1984, pp. 1-4, 1985, p. 2; Michael Przybylski and Drew Klacik, *The Ports of the Indiana Port Commission: Economic Impacts and Economic Development* (Indianapolis: Center for Urban Policy and the Environment, School of Public and Environmental Affairs, Indiana University, 1994); 32, 37, 38; Jeffersonville *Evening News,* July 28, 1989.

[9] Indianapolis *News,* June 16, 1987.

[10] Interview with Schram and Keck.

[11] Interview with Schram and Keck. See Appendix for complete list of commissioners.

[12] *Ibid.;* Indianapolis *Star,* December 20, 1988.

[13] *Ibid.;* IPC Minutes, May 31, 1984, p. 7; David G. Abraham to Ralph D. Gray, August 15, 1990.

[14] IPC *Annual Report,* 1984, p. 2; IPC Minutes, January 22, 1985; IPC Report of 1984 Significa, 3; IPC Minutes, August 27, 1984.

[15] IPC Minutes, April 26, 1984, p. 7, October 23, 1985, p. 5; IPC *Annual Report,* 1985, p. 3.

[16] See Chapter 6, note 10 for the litigation on harbor service charges. IPC Report of 1984 Significa, 2-3; IPC Minutes, January 22, 1985, pp. 3-4, May

30, 1984, p. 1; Indianapolis *Star,* October 5, 1989.

[17] The "sunset" process was designed "to establish a procedure for the responsible legislative evaluation of certain agencies and agency programs of state government to the end that (1) necessary agencies and agency programs be continued and unnecessary agencies and agency programs be terminated and (2) a restructuring of state government take place so that necessary agencies and agency programs be organized in a manner to provide efficient and effective government services." Indiana *Laws,* 1978, pp. 747, 754; Indiana Legislative Services Agency, Office of Fiscal and Management Analysis, *Sunset Performance Audit of Transportation Programs in Indiana* (Indianapolis, 1978), 81-83; interview with Schram and Keck.

### Epilogue, The Indiana Port Commission in the 1990s

[1] Indiana Port Commission, *Indiana Portside,* Spring 1995, p. 8.

[2] *Ibid.,* 9; Michael Przybylski and Drew Klacik, *The Ports of the Indiana Port Commission: Economic Impacts and Economic Development* (Indianapolis: Center for Urban Policy and the Environment, School of Public and Environmental Affairs, Indiana University, July 1994), p. 1. See also Laura Littlepage, Drew Klacik, and Michael Przybylski, with Seth Payton, *The Ports of the Indiana Port Commission: Economic Impacts and Economic Development* (Indianapolis: Center for Urban Policy and the Environment, School of Public and Environmental Affairs, Indiana University, January 1997).

[3] Przybylski and Klacik, *The Ports of the Indiana Port Commission, passim.*

[4] IPC, *Indiana Portside,* Summer 1995, p. 4.

[5] *Ibid.,* 8.

[6] *Ibid.,* 10.

[7] Indianapolis *Star,* June 18, 1995.

[8] "O'Bannon Welcomes Chemtrusion," Clark Maritime Centre, *MariTimes,* 5 (April 1996), [1]. See also "O'Bannon Welcomes New Joint Venture To Indiana Port," Indiana Port Commission Press Release, February 15, 1996, Indiana Historical Bureau Port History Files, Indiana State Archives.

[9] IPC, *Indiana Portside,* Spring 1996, p. 4.

[10] *Ibid.,* 7.

[11] *Ibid.*

[12] *Ibid.,* 15.

[13] *Ibid.,* Fall 1996, pp. 4-5.

[14] "Governor Bayh Announces State Support For New ConAgra Operations in Mount Vernon," Office of the Governor Press Release, July 31, 1996, IHB Port History Files, Indiana State Archives.

[15] IPC, *Indiana Portside,* Fall 1996, p. 14.

[16] *Ibid.,* Spring 1997, p. 10.

[17] *Ibid.,* 6. See Appendix for complete list of commissioners.

[18] Hammond *Times,* November 13, 1996. See also the brochure "On the occasion of Grand Opening for the William N. Kenefick Administration Building at Indiana's International Port/Burns Harbor in Portage, Indiana, November 12, 1996, 1:30 P.M.," IHB Port History Files, Indiana State Archives.

[19] IPC, *Indiana Portside,* Summer 1995, p. 3. See also "Tribute to the late William N. Kenefick," *Congressional Record,* Proceedings and Debates of the 104th Congress, First Session, September 6, 1995, v. 141, No. 137, p. E1708.

[20] IPC, *Indiana Portside,* Winter 1997, pp. 4-5.

[21] *Ibid.,* 8-9.

[22] Littlepage *et al., The Ports of the Indiana Port Commission,* 1. See also Gary *Post-Tribune,* December 12, 1996.

[23] Littlepage *et al., The Ports of the Indiana Port Commission,* 5-7.

[24] *Ibid.,* 8-11; IPC, *Indiana Portside,* Winter 1997, p. 9.

[25] Littlepage *et al., The Ports of the Indiana Port Commission,* 1.

[26] IPC, *Indiana Portside,* Winter 1997, pp. 10-11.

[27] *Ibid.,* 12-13.

[28] "Port Commission Authorizes Negotiations for Major Expansion of Port Operations," IPC Press Release, August 26, 1996, IHB Port History Files, Indiana State Archives.

[29] Indiana Stevedoring and Distribution Corporation Press Release, November 11, 1996, IHB Port History Files, Indiana State Archives. See also "Metals/Distribution Center Scheduled for Burns Harbor," *Skillings Mining Review,* November 16, 1996, p. 24.

[30] "Fednav liner service to move to Indiana port," *The Journal of Commerce,* November 19, 1996.

[31] IPC, *Indiana Portside,* Spring 1997, p. 5.

[32] *Ibid.,* 7.

[33] *Ibid.,* Winter 1995-1996, pp. 8-9.

[34] *Ibid.,* Summer/Autumn 1997, pp. 8-9.

[35] *Ibid.,* 3.

# A NOTE ON SOURCES

This study has been based upon three types of sources—primary and secondary sources and personal recollections. An extensive array of primary materials exists in the unprocessed Indiana Port Commission Collection in the Indiana State Archives: minutes of commission meetings, annual reports, and various other documents, reports, and correspondence. Of particular value are the feasibility studies compiled for each of the three ports by Sverdrup & Parcel and Associates, Inc. of St. Louis, as well as the periodic economic impact studies undertaken by different consultants. Some materials were assembled primarily by George A. Nelson, who donated them to the state and supplemented them with a long taped interview, a transcript of which was deposited in the Indiana Division of the Indiana State Library. The Nelson material, part of the Indiana Port Commission Collection, Indiana State Archives, also contains photographs, miscellaneous publications by a number of waterway associations, and considerable personal correspondence. Other primary sources include U.S. Army Corps of Engineers publications, especially the reports of the chief of engineers of the Corps, and various state and federal government records. A useful source about the Corps is John W. Larson, *Those Army Engineers: A History of the Chicago District, U.S. Army Corps of Engineers* (Chicago, 1979).

There is one basic publication regarding the Indiana Port Commission—Lawrence M. Preston's *The Port of Indiana: Burns Waterway Harbor* (Bloomington, Ind., [1970]), completed for distribution at the time of the Burns Harbor dedication in 1970. This booklet has been useful in developing sources and context.

The struggle to build this harbor, intimately involved with the history of the protection and development of the Indiana dunes as well as the background and early history of the Port Commission, has been discussed in a number of publications. Most useful, but slanted, is Kay Franklin and Norma Schaeffer, *Duel for the Dunes: Land Use Conflict on the Shores of Lake Michigan* (Urbana, Ill., 1983). See also J. Ronald Engel, *Sacred Sands: The Struggle for Community in the Indiana Dunes* (Middletown, Conn., 1983); Lynton K. Caldwell, Lynton R. Hayes, and Isabel M. MacWhirter, *Citizens and the Environment: Case Studies in Popular Action* (Bloomington, Ind., 1976); the autobiography of Senator Paul H. Douglas, *In the Fullness of Time* (New York, 1971); and briefer mentions of these subjects in works by and about Indiana politicians: Matthew E. Welsh, *View from the State House: Recollections and Reflections, 1961-1965* (Indianapolis, 1981); William J. Watt, *Bowen: The Years as Governor* (Indianapolis, 1981); and Henry Z. Scheele, *Charlie Halleck: A Political Biography* (New York, 1966). Two sources have been useful for biographical information about relevant individuals: Justin E. Walsh, gen. ed., *A Biographical Directory of the Indiana General Assembly*, Vol. 2, *1900-1984* (Indianapolis, 1984) and *Biographical Directory of the United States Congress, 1774-1989* (Washington, D.C., 1989).

Useful general works on the history of transportation include George

Rogers Taylor, *The Transportation Revolution, 1815-1860* (New York, 1951); *Transportation and the Early Nation* (Indianapolis, 1982); Louis C. Hunter, *Steamboats on the Western Rivers: An Economic and Technological History* (Cambridge, Mass., 1949); Jacques LesStrang, *The Great Lakes St. Lawrence System* (Harbor Island, Maple City, Mich., 1984); *Big Load Afloat: U.S. Domestic Water Transportation Resources* (rev. ed., Washington, D.C., 1973); and J. R. Whittaker, *Containerization* (2nd ed., Washington, D.C., 1975).

Interesting to collect, if not always the most useful, are personal recollections, or, better yet, on-the-job discussions of activities at the Indiana Port Commission and its far-flung domains. I have benefited from interviews with personnel at all three of the Indiana public ports, with some of the current and former commissioners, and many others, particularly staff members, political leaders from the 1960s and afterwards, and journalists who have covered the ongoing developments at the Indiana ports. Although not always specifically named in the text or cited in the notes, these sources have provided context and insights not otherwise available. Copies of my notes have been provided for the Indiana Historical Bureau's source files.

When the original research for this book was undertaken, many of the items used were in the Indiana Port Commission office. Since that time, many of these materials have been dispersed or deposited in the Indiana State Archives; the collection remains unprocessed to date. This collection is cited throughout the notes as Indiana Port Commission (IPC) Files, Indiana State Archives.

Since retrieval of sources was often quite difficult, the Indiana Historical Bureau created files of sources chapter by chapter. These are cited throughout the notes as Indiana Historical Bureau (IHB) Port History Files, Indiana State Archives. An alphabetical subject file of many sources was also created. Both of these files have been deposited in the Indiana State Archives to aid in further research by interested parties.

All Port Commission reports cited in this book are located in the IPC Files, Indiana State Archives. Minutes of the Indiana Board of Public Harbors and Terminals and the Indiana Port Commission are located in the vault of the Indiana State Archives.

## INDIANA PORT COMMISSION
### Commissioners and Chairmen

**Commissioners of the Indiana Port Commission**

| Commissioner | Political Party | Residence | Dates of Service | |
|---|---|---|---|---|
| James R. Fleming | Republican | Fort Wayne | 1961-1969 | Replaced by |
| Joseph N. Thomas | Republican | Gary | 1969-1975 | Replaced by |
| Harry F. Zaklan | Republican | Indianapolis | 1976-1985 | Replaced by |
| Arthur D. Hopkins | Republican | Liberty | 1985-1994 | Replaced by |
| Steven E. Chancellor | Republican | Evansville | 1994-1996 | Replaced by |
| H. C. "Bud" Farmer | Republican | Evansville | 1997-Current | |
| | | | | |
| Robert M. Schram | Democrat | Peru | 1961-1983 | Replaced by |
| Joe E. Robertson | Democrat | Brownstown | 1985-1991 | Replaced by |
| John D. Bottorff | Democrat | Seymour | 1991-Current | |
| | | | | |
| George A. Nelson | Democrat | Valparaiso | 1961-1975 | Replaced by |
| Quentin A. Blachly | Democrat | Valparaiso | 1976-1989 | Replaced by |
| William N. Kenefick | Democrat | Michigan City | 1989-1995 | Replaced by |
| Joseph E. Costanza | Democrat | Ogden Dunes | 1995-1997 | Replaced by |
| Steven R. Stemler | Democrat | Jeffersonville | 1997-Current | |
| | | | | |
| William E. Shumaker | Republican | Indianapolis | 1961-1974 | Replaced by |
| William S. Young | Republican | Plymouth | 1974-1984 | Replaced by |
| Martin H. Gross | Republican | Indianapolis | 1985-1985 | Replaced by |
| Robert L. Poor | Republican | Greencastle | 1986-1993 | Replaced by |
| Marvin E. Ferguson | Republican | Indianapolis | 1993-Current | |
| | | | | |
| Albert L. Yeager | Democrat | Michigan City | 1961-1964 | Replaced by |
| Henry R. Sackett | Democrat | Gary | 1964-1970 | Replaced by |
| William H. Keck | Democrat | Mount Vernon | 1970-1991 | Replaced by |
| N. Stuart Grauel | Democrat | Indianapolis | 1991-Current | |
| | | | | |
| William E. Babincsak | Democrat | Gary | 1975-1988 | Replaced by |
| R. Louie Gonzalez | Democrat | East Chicago | 1989-1993 | Replaced by |
| W. Ken Massengill | Democrat | Schererville | 1994-Current | |
| | | | | |
| Norman E. Pfau, Jr. | Republican | Jeffersonville | 1975-1995 | Replaced by |
| Mary Ann Fagan | Republican | Indianapolis | 1995-Current | |

## Chairmen of the Indiana Port Commission

Governor Matthew E. Welsh acted as chairman until the organization of the commission was completed.

| Chairman | Term of Office |
| --- | --- |
| James R. Fleming | April 10, 1961 - May 15, 1969 |
| Robert M. Schram | May 15, 1969 - June 15, 1969 |
| Joseph N. Thomas | June 15, 1969 - July 31, 1974 |
| William S. Young | August 1, 1974 - December 31, 1983 |
| William H. Keck | January 1, 1984 - April 25, 1984 (acting) |
| Quentin A. Blachly | April 26, 1984 - February 22, 1989 |
| William H. Keck | February 23, 1989 - February 8, 1991 |
| R. Louie Gonzalez | February 11, 1991 - September 17, 1993 |
| William N. Kenefick | October 25, 1993 - August 10, 1995 |
| N. Stuart Grauel | September 15, 1995 - Current |

# INDEX